SANDLING MEMORIES

by

Robin Ambr

"Far from the madding crowd's ignoble strife,
  Their sober wishes never learn'd to stray;
  Along the cool sequester'd vale of life
They kept the noiseless tenour of their way".

Gray's Elegy

i

ISBN 978-0-9537430-2-5

Printed in Great Britain by Scarbutts Printers, West Malling, Kent

DEDICATION

To Bob and June Corner, without whose
memories, help and encouragement this book
would have been the poorer.

ALREADY PUBLISHED

Boxley – The Story of an English Parish

Penenden Heath's Story

CONTENTS

Preface and Acknowledgements

Contributors

PREFACE AND ACKNOWLEDGEMENTS

This book is a companion to the earlier publication "Boxley – The Story of an English Parish" (the Boxley book). That includes much of Sandling's history, with specific chapters on the Abbey, the Lushingtons and the riverside. Daevid Hook's research for the Boxley book is again much used.

Sandling is but part of the large Boxley parish, and the stories told stretch from the riverside across to Boxley Abbey, and up from Ringlestone and Invicta Park to the foot of the Downs.

Several well-to-do families had their homes within Sandling and were the main landowners. Their lives and those of the farming, village and business communities have prompted many memories. Readers who might dip and skip around different chapters could be confused to come across apparently unexplained references to such as "green tops" and "cut-throat alley", but the answers do lie within. Sir Garrard Tyrwhitt-Drake's long name needed to be shortened, and though some local people used to call him "Twitty" he is here mostly called "Garrard".

The many people who have contributed their memories are acknowledged at the end of the book. Special mention has to be made of Bob and June Corner, who have not only re-lived their own times for us but have introduced many of their acquaintances who have been equally welcoming to recall the past, and often make precious family photos available. Peter Kirby has been a particularly great source of information and photographs.

Two authors have been generous in giving consent for their own material to be drawn upon. Vickie Harris, who wrote "The Story of Maidstone Zoo", and Robin Walton, who with Annie Ross-Davies wrote "Changing Fortunes" which told the story of Sandling Farm. Tony Webb, author of "Out of the Blue", provided valuable material for the wartime chapter.

As always, postcards have helped to illustrate the past. More generosity has been shown by collectors Irene Hale, Dorothy and Stuart Murray, Mary and Roger Birchall and Jean Allison in allowing their Sandling subjects to be copied and used. Maps have been reproduced with the kind permission of Ordnance Survey.

Some readers may find their own memories and understanding of facts at odds with what lies within. They are welcome to let the author know!

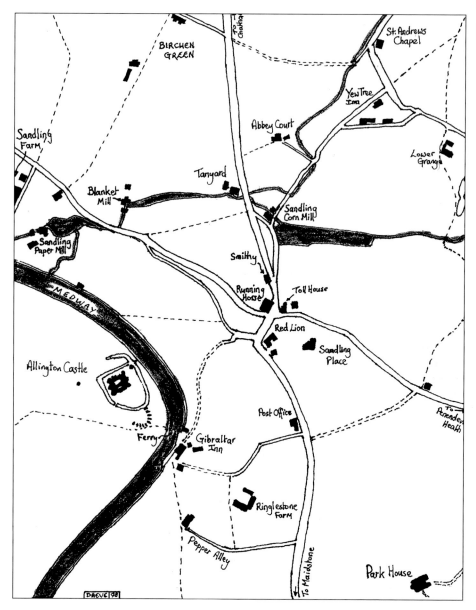

Sandling circa 1840.

(Daevid Hook)

CHAPTER 1

At the Crossroads

In days gone by the focal point of Sandling was The Running Horse pub and the meeting of roads which provided the routes north to Chatham, south to Maidstone, west to Aylesford, and east to Penenden Heath. One might also add north-east to Boarley. Today's jumble of flyover, underpass, slip roads and roundabout is in complete contrast to the simple crossroads which the nearby map of Sandling around 1840 shows.

The map gives us an introduction to features which have long since been swept away, such as the smithy, toll house and Red Lion Inn, which all stood close by The Running Horse. On a map of 1866 we see woodland stretching down to the Medway, not long afterwards to be felled and replaced by sandpits. The house Brooklyn has arrived to join Abbey Court on the road to Chatham.

The smithy was still shown on a map of 1908 but was not to survive for much longer. One of the last blacksmiths was a Mr Dadd who had five daughters by his first wife and then three sons by his second wife Elizabeth Fullagar. The incline close by where the smithy once stood was still being called Forge Hill by some people as late as the 1950s.

The Running Horse pub shown on the early maps is not The Running Horse that we know today. The original was a much simpler building built in 1732. Its name is said to come from the legend that a horse bolted from thereabouts and galloped to Boxley Abbey carrying strapped to its back the crucifix which in the hands of the monks became "The Holy Rood of Grace".

By the 1930s the old pub had seen its best days, and the increasing presence of motor vehicles was sometimes putting it in the line of fire of large buses and lorries negotiating their way past. Today's Running Horse was built about 1938 on land behind the old pub. When the new building was finished the old one was demolished.

In its smart re-incarnation the pub attracted a new clientele. One interesting group to meet there were pigeon fanciers, including local farmers George Brundle and Dennis Beeby, and policeman Tom Rumble. They would gather on a Friday night and load their boxed pigeons into a covered lorry which then drove off through the night to some far distant destination, believed once even to have been France. The birds were released on the Saturday morning and then there was the suspense and rivalry in seeing whose came home first, usually that same Saturday. The lawn behind the pub was used at one time to play bat and trap.

The brewers were Style and Winch, of whom Sir Garrard Tyrwhitt-Drake from Cobtree Manor was a director. He was a talented artist and drew and painted many of the brewery's inn signs, including at one time that for The Running Horse. A young Bob Corner (long associated with Tyland Farm) was requested to trot on a donkey in front of

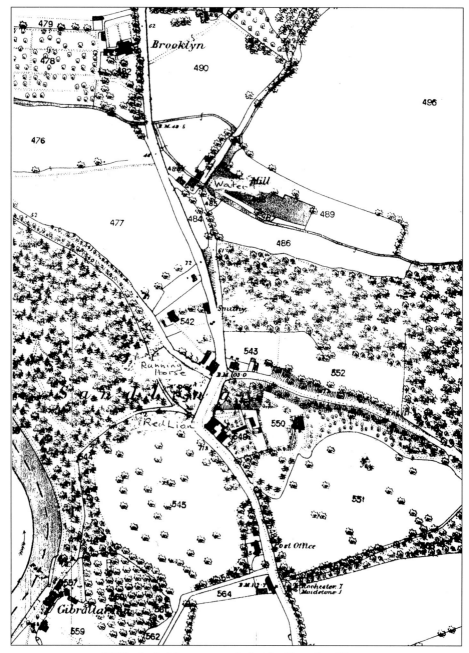

1866. A simple crossroads by the Running Horse.

The Running Horse circa 1910.

Cobtree Manor so that Garrard could study the creature's leg movements and try to get them right in his painting. Bob wasn't sure that he was that successful.

In the 1930s the road layout around The Running Horse was changed, with a new carriageway constructed to swing away to the west. The 1938 map shows the sweep of the new stretch beginning by the Sandling Place stables (where the Red Lion Inn once stood) and then just before Brooklyn joining the line of the old Roman road. All this created an island of land in front of The Running Horse which for some years became a playground for local children. Margaret McCarthy (nee Whale) remembers it as a bumpy area with a lot of sand which was ideal for scampering and riding bikes. She knew it as Green Island, whilst to others it was Cat Island or Monkey Island. As with much of Sandling, there were many sand martins to be seen. The area is now covered over as the pub's car park.

The 1938 map shows that the road to Aylesford no longer came off at a crossroads but had been moved further up. The sandpits close by were now mostly worked out and called "old". Opposite the junction of the new line of road will be seen a building named Club. This became better known as Sandling Village Hall and was used for a variety of activities over the years. Dick Blankley thought that it was first built in 1932. George Brundle, who ran Sandling Farm, was prominent with his wife Dorothy in running whist drives. Although perhaps looked upon as an "elderly pursuit", local youngsters were made welcome, as Tom Rumble's son Jack remembers. For some years the card players were fortified by refreshments supplied from Fred Smith's bakery up the Chatham Road.

Stuart Murray remembers the dances held in the hall which had a very springy floor. What they called the Wednesday Hop cost nine pence whilst the Saturday Hop cost one shilling. A five piece band came from Chatham and on these occasions Mrs Longley from the local grocery shop provided refreshments. But during the war years many local

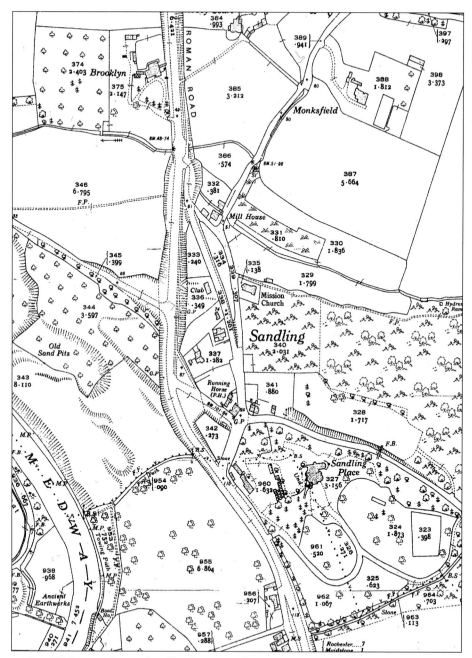

The 1938 map shows the Chatham Road now taking a wide sweep away from The Running Horse.

people were preferring to make their way to dances at The Star in Maidstone.

Then there was the baby clinic, with mums wheeling prams for quite long distances. Mrs Vaughan would push her twin boys all the way from Boxley village. Then the mums would make their return journeys with their allotment of welfare orange juice and powdered milk. Over the years the hall was run by a series of energetic people, in time as part of the Sandling Residents Association. There would be Christmas parties and many private celebration parties, whilst after 1971 Linda Ellis remembers an Old People's Club to provide tea and talking plus a few activities.

By the 1980s the hall was becoming rather dilapidated, and that was the time when developers were seeking permission to build the houses on what was eventually to become known as Bluebell Estate up the Chatham Road. This had been the site of Mr Smith's "Garden Bakery" and after that the site of an early out-of-town store selling mostly white electrical goods under the name of Oakhive. There was much opposition to the proposal, but the developers helped to overcome this by making a "substantial contribution" to the building of a new community hall.

For a while there were thoughts of having the new hall at the by then vacant Tyland Barn, but in 1993 the decision was made to dismantle and sell the old hall and build a new and modern one on the same site. Prominent amongst those organising all this was Rev. Joe Caley who had been vicar of East Farleigh and in retirement was living in one of the Bakery Cottages next to Tyland Barn. Joe was a Manxman, had been ordained into the priesthood at a young age, and saw service as an Army chaplain in the Far East. His wife Margaret was also very active in local affairs and various activities of the Residents Association. In recognition of Joe's efforts the new building when opened in October 1994 was named "Caley Hall".

Next we turn to the water mill in Boarley Lane, which having stood on its site for centuries appears consistently on maps of the area, and the Boxley book sets out much of its history. It always seems to have been a corn mill. Opinions vary as to when it ceased to be a working mill, some seeming to remember it still in action just after the Second War. The mill pond was created from the waters of the Boxley stream which runs through Cuckoo Wood, whilst another stream flows down the side of Boarley Lane. The whole area hereabouts is watery and with flooding having happened over the years.

The mill itself has sadly been burnt down. The Mill House next to it has been dated to the 1600s, and it is said that the front door step is a very worn old millstone. A Miss Newman who once lived there spoke of the ghost of "the old miller" pushing her, whilst a later owner Alan Moultrie once heard a strange voice singing. And then there is the tale of the ghost of an old woman crossing the road by the bridge just up the road. Another occupier at one time was Mr Pat Deeley, who is remembered as being Irish, and to the curiosity of some he apparently knitted his own socks.

Staying with the 1938 map, just east of the Club will be seen the Mission Church. Boxley parish, within which Sandling is but part, spreads over a wide area and the Church itself in Boxley village was not always easy to get to. Prior to 1914 there had been open air services, thought to be near The Yew Tree. Music was provided by an ocarina (defined as "flute like and egg-shaped") and later the curate Cecil Hilton played

The Mill House.

a portable harmonium. On another occasion some boys physically transported a proper harmonium. Then Mrs Roper from Harbourland House in Boxley obtained the use of the Mill House, though it seems more likely that the Mill itself was used. Set out below is a report from a parish magazine of 1916.

The Sandling Mission

"Certain members of the congregation at the Mill House having suggested that a Harvest Festival should be held there, one was arranged at rather short notice for Sunday evening, October 1st. The mill machinery had been taken out, and the place was in some disorder on Friday afternoon before, but Mr Parkes turned to and soon made things better, and Mrs Deeley kindly scrubbed the floor, and everything was ready for the decorators on Saturday afternoon. A fine lot of flowers, fruit and vegetables had been sent, and the decorators, who included amongst their number several members of the Parkes family, Mrs Mannering, Mrs Roper, Miss Corrie, Mr Baker, Mr Brunger, and one or two more, did wonders in transforming a not very beautiful interior so that it looked very pretty indeed. A trestle table was used to display the gifts to better advantage, and almost every available spot had some flowers or something in it. The room normally will hold about 50 comfortably, but it was found possible to squeeze in over 80 that night and some followed the service from outside. Mr F. Parkes brought his violin, and the singing was very hearty. A collection was made on behalf of the West Kent Hospital and realised 30s. The fruit, etc., was kindly taken in next day to the Lady Howard de Walden Hospital by Mr Fullagar, where it was well received, and there was especial competition amongst the wounded soldiers for a fuchsia plant which had formed part of the decorations. The Mission has lately received some splendid presents. Mr E. Hughesman designed, made in heart oak, and presented a reading desk. It is a noble piece of furniture, and supplies a real want. Mr Parkes has given a Bible. Mrs Roper some very fine sacred pictures of the Fitzroy series. We are not quite draught proof yet, but we hope that before the winter sets

7

in we shall be quite comfortable. Everybody is very helpful; Mr and Mrs Deeley do everything they can, without being asked, to make us comfortable, and all the congregation seem ready to help to the best of their ability".

Then the Parish magazine of 1926 is referring to the "unsatisfactory and inadequate accommodation for the church services at Sandling". Steps were needed to remedy this and to provide "at the same time accommodation for the social and recreational life of this rapidly developing neighbourhood". Things soon began to happen, Mr Randall Mercer from Sandling Place gave some land on the corner of Cuckoo Wood and local people gave generously to a Building Fund. It was not long before the new Mission Church was up and running. The structure was mostly metal and there were none better to erect it than the local firm of Parkes Brothers just down the Chatham Road who built and repaired carriages and motor vehicles. Later generations came to call it with some irreverence the "Tin Tabernacle".

The usual services were held, but people seem to remember best of all the Sunday Schools. Stuart Murray remembers these in the 1930s with Mrs Kitney playing the harmonium. The Vicar would look in sometimes and ask what hymns they would like to sing. The boys always wanted "Onward Christian Soldiers", at which Mrs Kitney would sigh and complain that she would rather play something different. Stuart also remembers the Christmas parties when the children all walked up to Park House in Boxley village, then back again holding torches and clutching nuts and oranges. A Sunday school teacher in his time was Miss Farrow, daughter of Mr Farrow from Monksfield.

Margaret McCarthy remembers the 1950s when the Mission still had gas lighting. Among the teachers were Mrs Conway and her husband, and Margaret recalls Mr Conway getting the lamps to work, and proclaiming at each one "Let there be Light". Other teachers at this time were Mrs Hobday, Margaret Bray from Abbey Cottages, and a very young Pat McCabe who was by then living at Malta Cottage, to where she would invite groups of the children to have tea. Barbara Steadman remembers a very large fireplace in the lounge.

For some years the Mission was very well supported by local people. Fred Owen was a gardener at the Abbey and devoted much time to getting the Mission ready for services, and for Harvest Festivals was to be seen wheeling along barrowloads of produce. But the passing years brought an increase in the number of people having motor cars and well able to get to Boxley Church. The congregation dwindled and closure was the sad result. Jack Bradford from Tyland Lane had remained a regular, but with typical understanding remarked "Don't keep it open just for me". It was some time in the 1960s that the Mission closed, and those local churchgoers still without transport had a parish bus to take them to Boxley. The Mission was demolished and a bungalow now stands on the site.

Increasingly from 1930 the crossroads near The Running Horse were extremely busy with traffic, coming to a climax in the 1950s. North and South was the rush between Maidstone and Chatham. East and West the route between Aylesford and Bearsted became in effect an early Maidstone by-pass to avoid the traffic jams there. Traffic from London was diverted down Teapot Lane at Ditton, through Aylesford village and along

A Nativity play in the Mission 1951. Standing second from right is Danny Jarmann with Bridget Conway on his right and Eileen Hook at his feet. *(Eileen Hook)*

Forstal Road to pass by The Running Horse on its way past Penenden Heath. Weekend traffic was particularly heavy with people making for the coast and later returning.

All this traffic required control by the police. Bob Corner had been persuaded to become a special constable and was on duty on the Forstal Road corner with regular P.C. Tom Rumble near The Running Horse, each wearing white capes. There was a lull and Tom slipped up to the village hall to relax and smoke his beloved pipe. Then a message came that the Superintendent was on his way to see how things were going. Tom hastily crammed his pipe into his pocket and returned to duty.

It was now dark, and Bob Corner from his own position saw a red glow which grew brighter and brighter. Both Tom's pocket and coat were alight and had holes burnt in them. According to son Jack Rumble, this happened more than once. On this occasion Tom did not dare tell his wife but got a kindly local lady to do the necessary repairs.

One Sunday the traffic queues were particularly bad, and Bob Corner remembers a Sergeant arriving to say that there were jams all the way back to Penenden Heath. The advice and remedy was simple. "North and south won't like it but stop them and give the coast traffic a full five minutes".

Time now to move west from The Running Horse and visit Sandling Farm.

The Running Horse in 2012. Now viewed across a dual carriageway.

The Running Horse Restaurant circa 1970.

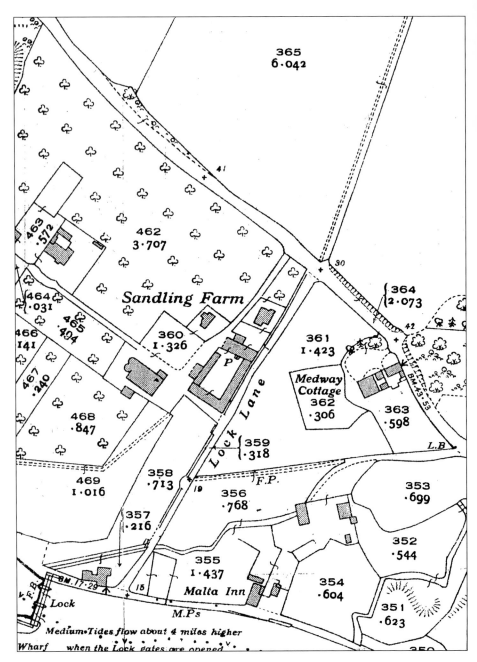

A map of 1938.

11

CHAPTER 2

Sandling Farm

This farm for many years occupied what is now the site of the Museum of Kent Life and was part of Tyrwhitt-Drake's Cobtree Estate. Much of the information contained here comes by kind permission of Robin Walton who included the farm's story in the book "Changing Fortunes" which he co-wrote with Annie Ross-Davies.

The farmhouse which is open to visitors at the Museum was built in the 1700s with later additions. What is now the Museum's café was built in the late 1800s as a more stylish farmhouse. We do best to refer to them as the old and the new farmhouses.

In 1925 a twenty-two years old George Brundle was taken on by Garrard Tyrwhitt-Drake to farm as tenant at both Sandling and Tyland farms. Garrard was hesitant in offering the tenancy to such a young man, but Garrard's mother said "Give the young man a chance". So began George's long working life at Sandling which was to last until 1980.

George came from a family of nine in Dulwich, and two of his brothers were killed in the First War. His father ran a successful metal business and agreed to back George financially for two years on condition that he employed a manager with farming skills and experience. Bob Corner's father Bill Corner, who was working for Robert Veitch on neighbouring Cossington Farm, heard about the job and decided to take it. So began a long working association. We shall hear more of Bill later when we delve into memories of Tyland Farm.

Although the Oast and hop pickers' huts at the Museum might make you think otherwise, George never grew hops commercially. The Oast was evidence of activity in earlier years, whilst the Museum acquired the huts from elsewhere. George made use of the roundels for fattening cockrels and storing potatoes. He kept Friesian and Jersey cows for milking, and would deliver milk locally. Ann Nissen from the green top houses in Chatham Road remembers him calling post-war and ladling it out in one pint or two pint measures. Milking was carried out very early in the morning and again in the afternoon. A very young Stuart Murray (living in one of the houses opposite the green tops) was very anxious to begin learning his farming skills. His mother would wake him at 5.30 am and he would walk to Sandling Farm where George very kindly taught him how to milk.

George kept one bull to perform necessary functions with the cows. Sheep and pigs were also kept, the pigs being fed on swill collected from sources ranging from pubs and cafes to Allington Castle across the river. A grown-up Stuart Murray, by now doing his own farming, would walk a couple of sows held by string all the way to Sandling Farm where George would let him "put them to the boar". The sows might be left with the

George Brundle at the wheel and Bill Corner behind. (Bob Corner)

boar for a whole day at the princely sum of one shilling.

Arriving as a milking stockman in 1949 was Joe Relf, who lived at Stream Cottages with his wife and four sons. As his son Raymond remembers, Joe was remarkably devoted to his work, never once taking a day off, not even on Christmas Day. He would be up at 5 a.m. for the morning milking, and when his sons married he brought this forward to 3 a.m. and the afternoon milking to 11 a.m. so that he could attend the ceremony. Even if ill he would still struggle to work. He developed a rupture, which Raymond described "as big as a football". He refused an operation but did agree to have a truss fitted, but having got home he cast it aside and never touched it again.

One of Joe's specialities was castration, and his victims would include animals at the zoo. He would often act as an informal vet. Pat Sandford heard tell of Joe staying up all night with a sick cow, and that when the creature died Joe was reduced to tears. And if one of the cows was in calf he would stay with it day and night until there had been a safe delivery. Mrs Relf and the boys saw no holidays or family outings, though there were trips to The Running Horse where they would all gather round the piano for a sing song.

Remembering that George was also tenant of Tyland Farm, it was there that cereals were grown, and some cattle grazed. By 1927 he was married to Dorothy and they settled down to life together for many years at the old farmhouse, which they called Sandling Farm Cottage. The new farmhouse was excluded from the tenancy and was let

Sandling Farmhouse in 2010. Now the Museum café.

instead to people such as a prominent eye surgeon Mr Heath and was called Sandling Farmhouse. Dorothy followed the age-old tradition of a farmer's wife in looking after the chickens who yielded great supplies of eggs. It is said that she always fancied living in the grander Sandling Farmhouse.

George always worked alongside his farmhands especially for haymaking and harvesting, when he would bring out a barrel of cider for refreshment. Wally Bishop, who worked on the farm in the early 1940s, described George as a "true gentleman". The men called him "Guv'nor". Wally remembers the harvest suppers held in a shed opposite the old farmhouse with George and Dorothy providing much food and drink. Another memory Wally has is of having to deal with cows' backsides. He would tie half a hessian sack round his waist as protection, and wear his cap back to front in order to get all the closer to the work in hand. Yet another memory he has is of being so proud to be allowed to use the Welsh cob mare to rake hay into rows ready for loading into the hay wagons.

George once travelled all the way to Wales to acquire some shire horses. Unimaginably he brought these home first by train to Chatham and then walked them to Tyland Farm. Robin Walton referred to these "good-natured magnificent horses" which were used for ploughing, drilling and harvesting, and for pulling dung carts and wagons. In the 1930s George bought his first tractor. Then in 1954 his first combine harvester, which was kept at Tyland Farm. When it needed to be moved between farms it was necessary to inform the police. And all this time there was much orchard land around the farm bearing all manner of fruit, with cherries being the main crop.

A view of the oast in 2012, with Sandling Farm Cottage far right.

Around 1960 the Maidstone By-pass arrived and denied easy access between the two farms, and George had to pass along the river bank and under the arch which carried the motorway over the Medway. George seems to have continued farming until about 1980, by which time he was seventy-seven. In 1964 Garrard had died, by his will leaving Sandling Farm and the rest of his Cobtree Estate in trust "for the benefit of the people of Maidstone". It took some time to organise things but the creation of a museum was put in hand and opened in 1985. The book "Changing Fortunes" tells the story.

George and Dorothy had no children, and whilst continuing to live at Sandling Farm Cottage in retirement, George delighted in sharing his wisdom with the Young Farmers, and talking to young visitors to the Museum. His wisdom and lifetime experiences were also invaluable to those setting up the Museum, restoring buildings, and collecting exhibits. George died in 2001 and there is an oak tree planted to his memory at the Museum.

Sandling Farm Cottage in 2012.

George Brundle.   *(Robin Walton)*

Two old views of Cobtree.

CHAPTER 3

Cobtree

As Forstal Road takes you over the motorway, towards Aylesford and leaving the Museum of Kent Life behind, there lies on the right the entrance lodge to Garrard Tyrwhitt-Drake's old home Cobtree Manor. In 1881 the tenant was a very interesting man William Trousdell, of whom his grandson Jim Trousdell provided the following information.

He was born in Ireland in 1841 and was the fifteenth child in a family of nineteen. He enlisted in the British Army in 1862, was made a sergeant by 1864, and in 1866 was given a commission in the 7th Hussars. Fast progress. His regiment was posted to the cavalry barracks in Maidstone, of which the officers' mess still survives as The White Rabbit pub/restaurant. It was at Maidstone that he met his future wife Ellen Whatman, a daughter of the fourth James Whatman of Vinters. They married at Boxley church in 1875 and were to have twelve children. As Jim Trousdell recalled, grandfather was a penniless Irishman and of a completely different social background to his wife. How he was ever allowed to marry her was always a mystery to the family. No doubt the charm of the Irish!

William Trousdell resigned his commission in 1876 and much against his wife's wishes he took up farming, at first in Ireland. That failed and the family came back to Maidstone and he rented Cobtree Farm. He was there for some seventeen years, but this enterprise seems to have failed also. The family made a final move to live at Maryland, a house in Vinters Road long gone which belonged to the Whatmans. William died in 1918 but his widow survived until 1942. Of their many children, three sons were decorated for bravery in the First War, one daughter Evelyn became a much loved Boxley Parish Nurse, whilst another daughter Kate married Frank Balston to forge a link between two of Maidstone's prominent papermaking families.

Garrard's mother.

It was in 1896 that Garrard's father Hugh took over as tenant, and in 1904 bought the house and various neighbouring farms. The big house was further extended and improved, having been shown on early maps as Cobtree Hall. Hugh chose to name it Cobtree Manor. The estate became known as the Cobtree Manor Estate comprising Cobtree Farm itself, Sandling Farm and Tyland Farm and covering in all some three hundred acres. The oldest part of Cobtree Manor was Elizabethan, no doubt first built as a farmhouse. Attractive Flemish gables had been added at some time. Hugh doubled the size by building extensions and the result was a most imposing structure.

Hugh died in 1908 and the estate passed to his son Garrard, who in 1899 had gone to live and work on a ranch in Argentina. There his love of animals grew to a lifelong passion. He also became fascinated by circus life and back home in England went touring with his own "Garrard's Royal Circus" for which he was the ringmaster. His surname was not used because relatives objected to the family being associated with such an outfit.

We have a separate chapter to tell about the zoo he created, and he had begun collecting wild animals prior to the First War. The arrival of that war found him unfit for military service and he was rather unceremoniously put into the Labour Corps. Then more fittingly he was transferred to the Veterinary Corps wherein he rose to the giddy height of corporal.

Peace came and in 1925 at the age of 44 he married his wife Edna, driving her away from Boxley Church in an open carriage. One of Garrard's sayings was to the effect that a Tyrwhitt-Drake would never walk if he could ride a horse or drive in a carriage. And he wrote once "That everyone who was anyone, or who was not if they had sufficient money, drove in a carriage and pair or on special occasions in a coach and four". His widowed mother continued living at Cobtree Manor (dying in 1934 aged 85) and so the newly married couple started their time together at Sandling Farmhouse.

Too much has been written about Garrard's civil and public life to warrant overmuch repetition. To have been mayor of Maidstone on twelve occasions and to have been knighted in 1936 during the brief reign of Edward VIII says a great deal. He held many directorships, not least with the brewers Style & Winch. Let us rather recount some memories of this remarkable man.

As carriages gave way increasing to motor vehicles, so Garrard succumbed and was to be seen driving a yellow Rolls Royce which local people dubbed "the yellow peril". He would drive into Maidstone for his morning shave, sometimes with a tame cheetah as passenger. Rosemary Curtiss-Fuller recalls being enlisted to hold the creature's reins whilst Garrard was inside with his barber.

With one exception he was against hunting of any kind, but he did enjoy the chase. At 8 a.m. on a Sunday Bill Corner would be out on the estate tying a dead rabbit to a length of string and sprinkling aniseed over it. Then son Bob Corner would drag the corpse around on horseback to leave a trail. At the end of the trail the rabbit was tied high in a tree. Then the chase was on, led by the beagles who obviously got there before Garrard. Once he arrived to where the yelping dogs were gathered round the tree, then the carcase was cut down for the dogs to "enjoy".

But there is a twist to these proceedings. Netta Jarmann's son Danny from the Chatham Road Lodge would skin a rabbit, put a brick inside the skin and drag that around in a completely different direction to the one laid by Bill and Bob Corner. The beagles and everybody else were duly confused.

Vickie Harris in her book "The Story of Maidstone Zoo" puts it nicely about

19

Garrard that "as he grew older he became ever more thrifty". P.C. Tom Rumble persuaded Bob Corner to become a special constable, and he was sworn in before Garrard and Lady Edna, who were both magistrates. Lady Edna suggested a little celebration with whisky macs, which caused Garrard to huff and puff at his best whisky being so used. Alan Veitch from Cossington Farm was allowed to fish in the lake, but upon condition that any caught (usually roach) were handed over to be fed to the penguins. Though against hunting, Garrard did relent once a year to allow a group of local farmers to shoot foxes on the estate, which were after all a general nuisance.

It has been mentioned that he was a talented artist, and he used that skill to illustrate books which he wrote, and in producing his own Christmas cards. And The Running Horse was not the only Style & Winch pub for which he painted the inn sign.

One of Garrard's favourite spots on the estate was a cascade of water from the western end of the large lake which nowadays lies in the south-east corner of the golf course. The brick structure can still be seen. In one severe winter in the late 1930s the lake froze over and local people came to enjoy skating. Stuart Murray remembers cars parked by the edge in the evening with their lights on to illuminate the scene. During another severe winter postwar one of Garrard's beloved Royal Cream ponies fell through the ice and was drowned. It was several weeks before it could be recovered. The ponies were allowed to roam free and were allegedly descended from those once owned by Queen Victoria. They were sometimes lent for London pantomimes when they would come on stage pulling Cinderella's coach.

Was it ice on this lake or another in the neighbourhood that Charles Dickens told of falling though? At any event, it was a much earlier occupier of Cobtree Manor named William Spong from whom Dickens sought and received kind help in his wet and frozen state. The incident understandably stuck in Dickens' mind, and Cobtree Manor is said to be the Manor Farm of Pickwick Papers; Mr Spong the inspiration for the kind-hearted Mr Wardle; and the estate the setting for Dingley Dell. The name Dingley may well be a twist upon Sandling and Boxley, whilst the Blue Lion of Pickwick Papers was probably in Dickens' mind the local Red Lion Inn. Garrard amused himself by seeking to recreate "Dingley Dell" by his cascade. Members of the Dickens Fellowship used to delight in paying visits to Cobtree and imagining some of the events of Pickwick Papers taking place there.

The Royal Cream ponies. *(Ronald White)*

And again, pulling Cinderella's coach. *(Vickie Harris)*

The Dickens Fellowship visit Cobtree.   *(Vickie Harris)*

The Lodge in Forstal Road in 2012.

The lodge house which began this chapter used to be home to a general zoo keeper Reg Yardley. Lady Edna would pass to his wife any spare carpeting, and Mrs Yardley would simply lay each new arrival on top of the last one, so that in time there were five carpets sitting one on top of the other. When it was necessary for woodworm treatment to be carried out, the disbelieving workmen simply refused to remove these layers upon layers.

Further up the drive from the entrance lodge is Garden Lodge, once home to the head gardener Edgar Hussey and his wife. She used at one time to man the zoo ticket office which stood close by.

There still stands near Cobtree Manor the old butchery, where meat was cut up for the many hungry zoo animals. The slaughterman was given a humane killer, but still seemed to find it necessary to use it in conjunction with a hammer. He was to be seen with his clothing covered in blood, but come Saturday night all smartened up with a bowler hat and ready for his regular trip to Maidstone's delights.

The zoo was to close in 1959 and Garrard died five years later at the age of 83. Those final years were obviously difficult, and the arrival of the motorway had a big impact. It seems he pestered the County Council to keep changing the paint on one stretch of fencing. Land was lost to roadworks, and other land sold. Lady Edna was annoyed when the timber firm was set up in Forstal Road and she organised the planting of the long row of conifers just up from the elephant house in order to create a screen.

Lady Edna died in 1992 aged 89. She was some twenty years younger than Garrard. There had been no children. She had continued to live in Cobtree Manor, but the grand old house had seen better times. Maybe Garrard should have spent some money on it, for much of the Elizabethan portion had developed serious dry rot and beetle infestation. Tragically the drawing room, library, main hall, breakfast room, four bedrooms and three bathrooms all had to be demolished. Only the dining room remained. Then around the year 2000 Robert Lawty purchased the long lease and to his enormous credit carried out huge renovation works. Cobtree Manor was saved, though much smaller in size.

Although prone to watch his pennies, there is no doubting Garrard's generosity in leaving the Cobtree Manor estate in trust for the benefit of local people. One just needs to mention the municipal golf course and the country park. In Cobtree Manor Park visitors can see the odd relic of zoo years. The dogs' graveyard can still be found, close by a pond up from the elephant house. Ranger Eva Durling has custody of the broken top half of one intriguing stone inscribed "To a dog Jack, found on a Boer farm in the Transvaal in 1901". What story lies behind that? The graveyard also has an unusual guest in Garrard's favourite chimpanzee Martha.

Although his parents lie buried in Boxley churchyard, Garrard himself was buried in Maidstone cemetery. He had always planned to be borne there in a carriage pulled by his Royal Cream ponies, but they had long gone. It is said that his body was embalmed.

But the Cobtree lands survive, seeking agreement to words in Pickwick Papers that "There ain't a better spot o' ground in all of Kent".

The dining room at Cobtree. (Irene Hales)

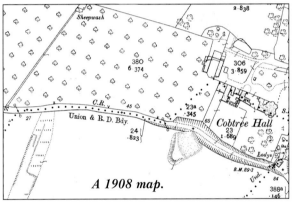

A 1908 map.

The restored sheepwash, now within Cobtree Country Park.

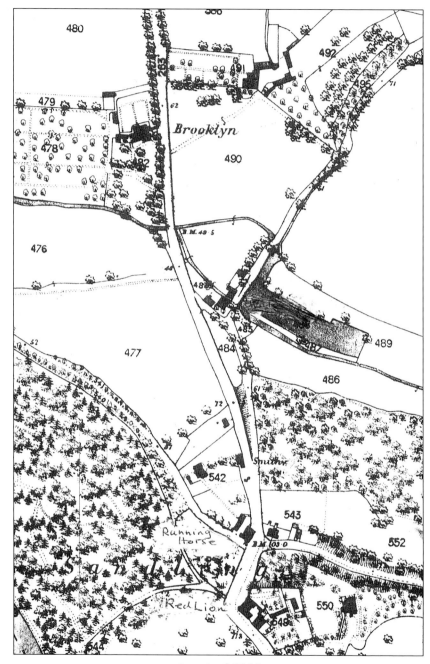

A map of 1866

CHAPTER 4

Brooklyn and Abbey Court

Returning to The Running Horse we now travel north towards the foot of Bluebell Hill. The 1866 map shows us passing the smithy and over where two streams meet to pass under the then much narrower road. This flow of streams was to power at one time two further mills before joining the Medway close by the Malta.

We come to the house Brooklyn, whose extensive grounds suggest farming activity in association with it once, though it would not appear to have been built as a farmhouse. Memories are very much more recent, and in the late 1930s Stuart Murray recalls a Colonel Murray living there and having two or three maids. During the war it was requisitioned by the Army who had begun their tenure at Sandling Park further down towards Maidstone. By 1950 Allan Phillips the builder was living there, and then Mr Tonna arrived and opened Veglios Restaurant. Later still the arrival of the motorway invited the addition of many motel buildings to the rear. Still more roadworks led in

1992, and a large culvert is constructed to take stream water under the new carriageways.
(Alan Moultrie)

26

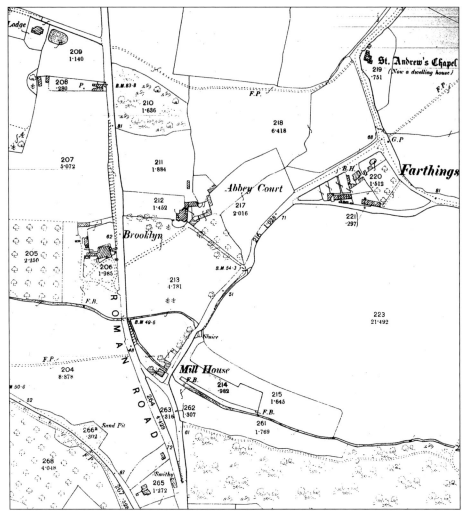

1897. Note the streams from Cuckoo Wood and Boarley meeting to pass under the road below Brooklyn.

Two views of Brooklyn. Above circa 1930 and below circa 1990. *(Irene Hales)*

1991 to the sad demolition of a building which held a lot of happy social memories for Maidstone people. Jump to 2012 and the large site is being developed as a car showroom and associated buildings.

Turning to the 1897 map we see north of Brooklyn the pair of Brooklyn Cottages which like the big house itself were to disappear with modern road widening.

Opposite Brooklyn there still stands Abbey Court, once the farmhouse to Abbey Court Farm. Up until the Dissolution of the Monasteries in the 1500s the monks of Boxley Abbey had built up large landholdings in the area. Much of their land passed to the Wyatts and then in time passed to their relatives the various Lords Romney. Indeed, each Lord Romney became the Lord of the Manor. In 1890 Lord Romney sold by auction the Boxley Abbey Estate which included Abbey Court Farm, Abbey Farm and Boarley Farm.

A deeds map of 1891 shows within the dark outlines the extent of Abbey Court Farm in the hands of Alfred Jarrett. Along the south boundary runs Chatham Road, and along the west boundary runs Tyland Lane, neither to have any houses built along their lengths until the 1920s. In the top north-west corner stand Abbey Court cottages. At the east corner the corn mill and mill pond are part of the farm.

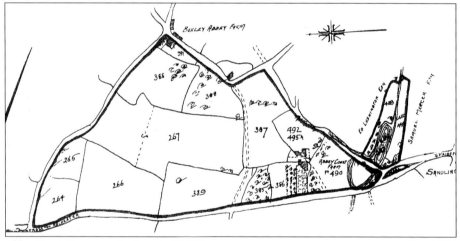

Abbey Court Farm on a deeds map of 1891. (*Les Ellis*)

Particularly from 1920 Abbey Court was known to local people as the hospitable home of Dr Constant Ponder and his wife and family. He and his wife invited a mix of admiration and surprise by having their many children walk and run around in bare feet, this being thought good for them. Dr Ponder rose to become Kent's Medical Officer for Health.

In the 1940s Stuart Murray was starting out on his farming career and renting some of Brooklyn's land to graze sheep and cattle. Dr Ponder kindly allowed him to use the old barns to house animals. Dr Ponder had converted the main barn, which dated back to the 1700s, into his own music room. Around 1928 a group of local musicians were looking for somewhere to meet, and Dr Ponder generously made the place available to them. They became known as The Old Barn Orchestra. Many of the Ponder family variously joined string and wind sections, whilst Mrs Ponder made sure that coffee was available during the break, sometimes with the assistance of a maid in cap and apron. Particularly in winter the players assembling for rehearsals had to negotiate a walk in the dark across a muddy farmyard. The barn was none too warm, and brave souls sitting to listen were perched on a sofa wrapped in rugs. There was one occasion when a cow wandered into the yard outside, put her head in at the door, and at a crucial stage in a Haydn symphony mooed very loudly.

The Old Barn.   *(Sylvia Coomber)*

That story, and information, comes from a history of the orchestra written in 1970. In it Dr Ponder's son Dr Dick Ponder recalled how as a small boy at an orchestral practice he went to fetch a music stand from a dark shed alongside the barn. He identified the stand by touch but thought it unusually heavy. When brought into the light it was seen to support a roosting hen which flew squawking over the players' heads and settled under the piano.

The orchestra ceased using the barn in 1949, Dr Constant Ponder died in 1955 and his wife in 1963. Their son Dr Richard Ponder and his wife made Abbey Court their home, and then some time in the 1950s another local group was in need of a base. This was Maidstone's Youth Theatre. Reflecting back in their mature years, old members realise just how generous the Ponders were, never making any charge for the use of the barn, not even for electricity. It was still a muddy walk to get there, until the young people set to and laid a concrete path. Dr Ponder praised this as being "nice – there is now no need to walk through farmyard what have you". But it was still necessary to kick chicken and the odd rat out of the way.

Stage make-up was applied in the Ponders' downstairs toilet, whilst at one time the girls would change in the dining room, going up when the call came "We've finished!". The boys would struggle to change in a shed behind the barn, Sylvia Coomber once having to help one of them get his trousers off. In time, with some outside help, they built a brick Green Room.

Sylvia remembers a few of them working late in the barn one New Year's Eve, and needing to find Dr Ponder in the house to borrow something. They found a party in full swing, and he insisted that they have a gin and orange. Unfortunately he forgot the gin and they struggled to down neat orange squash. Mrs Ponder, who had trouble pronouncing her r's, said "If I'd known you were needing to do things you could have used our spare woom, though it is full of wubbish".

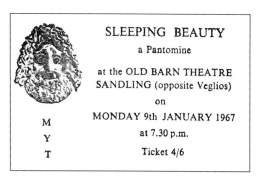

SLEEPING BEAUTY

a Pantomine

at the OLD BARN THEATRE
SANDLING (opposite Veglios)

on

MONDAY 9th JANUARY 1967

at 7.30 p.m.

Ticket 4/6

M
Y
T

Performance licences and other official requirements were strictly necessary, but one year the Council chose to refuse renewal. The young people carried on regardless, and Chris Norris remembers what happened next. A performance was in full swing in front of an audience of six people. Suddenly the door was flung open and in marched two men wearing gabardine macs and flanked by two burly policemen. There were several police cars outside. The performance stopped in bewildered fashion, whilst the officials went around with torches looking into dark corners. The police seemed bemused, maybe having expected a den of vice. The evening was abandoned, but the Youth Theatre continued to use the barn with no further harassment. Apart from many serious productions, pantomimes were put on with children in mind. These would run across two weeks and with matinees. The barn could hold an audience of some seventy-five. They were very happy days for the Youth Theatre, members often concluding rehearsals with a walk up to The Yew Tree for refreshment. Dr Richard Ponder retired in 1973, having had his surgery in Aylesford and seeing to the medical needs of many

Sandling people. He left the area, and not long after the Youth Theatre re-located.

And we must not forget the lake which the family had enlarged. Local children were allowed to swim during the summer, whilst in winter Peter Kirby remembers the lake freezing thick and dozens of people taking to it until late into the night. And Sir John Best-Shaw from the Abbey was given permission to fish there, and no doubt others as well.

Memories will long remain of two generations of the Ponder family who generously shared Abbey Court, and provided kindness and hospitality to many organisations and people.

The Ponder family at Abbey Court c. 1932. John, Dick, Audrey, Tony, Nan, Mrs. Ponder and Dr. Constant Ponder, Geoffrey, Brenda.

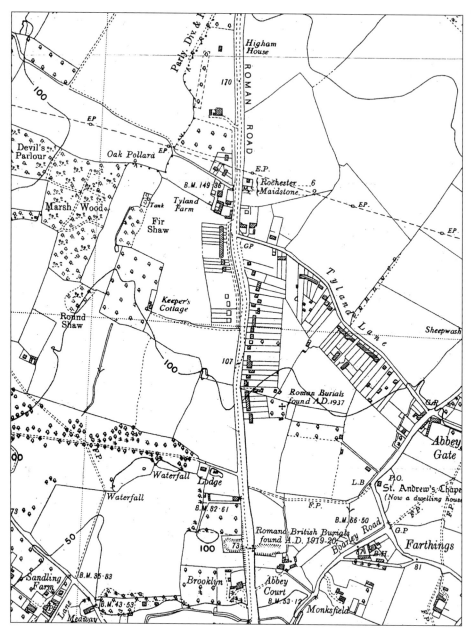

A map of 1947.

CHAPTER 5

Up the Chatham Road

Continuing north on the old road after our visits to Brooklyn and Abbey Court we would have passed on our left the pair of Brooklyn Cottages and soon after that the Chatham Road entrance to Cobtree. There beside a large pond stood the Lodge, which became the home to a zoo keeper Ernie Gates and his wife. At the time of writing the Lodge still stands in a derelict state, marooned close by junction 6 of the M20. Memories of life in the Lodge and memories of the zoo will come in later chapters.

Across the road from the Lodge used to be sandpits, once run by the builders Clarke & Epps. A Mr Robson from Tyland Lane used to work there, and basically you went in and helped yourself and he took the money. Brenda Steadman recalls the many sand martins there.

Remembering the 1891 map shown earlier, to left and right beyond the Lodge and up to the junction with Tyland Lane were no houses, just farmland. It was during the 1920s that houses began to spring up on the east side, with a lot of well-known characters to go with them. Stuart Murray's parents were amongst the new arrivals. His father Jim Murray was a plumber by trade, but he had a hobby of keeping both pigs and sheep, building pig styes at the bottom of his garden. In 1932 he bought a lot of land in the vicinity of where the 1947 map shows Roman burials being found. In fact it was Stuart who unearthed the objects in 1937 whilst digging down to create a deeper overflow for a pond. On part of the land which he had bought Jim built a new house at the southern end of the stretch of houses, and named it Rochester Meadow. In time Rochester Meadow was demolished for still more road works.

Brooklyn Cottages.   *(Irene Hales)*

Stuart was inevitably delegated to help care for his father's growing collections of pigs and sheep which were now enjoying some large fields. Stuart fell in love with farming, left school at fourteen, acquired cattle and sheep of his own and began by renting fields from Colonel Murray at Brooklyn. The traffic in wartime was not too bad and he was able to walk a couple of cows up and across the road to milk them back home for family needs. The other cows were left suckling heifers and calves.

When new neighbours Don and Margaret Dracup arrived in the 1960s Jim Murray was retired but still enjoying his fields and animals. Mrs Murray used to summon him by ringing an old school bell. When Les and Linda Ellis moved into Atherton in 1971 an elderly neighbour quickly introduced himself as Mr Pilkington, "but call me Pilkie". He remembered the houses being first built and told of a stream running down their side of the road which people had to cross to get to their homes. Les and Linda (whose house was built in 1923) had a well in their garden and understood the water table to be very high. The Maidstone Water Works company had been formed in 1860 and Mr Pilkington seemed to have heard of them in those early days extracting water from the area and transporting it down to Maidstone by cart.

Another well-known resident was Miss Emily Shrubsole, known to her family as Emmy. Her niece Anna Wood remembers her having an impish sense of humour and joining wholeheartedly in family party games. Her brother was Frederick "Tom"

By 1961 there is a dual carriageway and the by-pass bridge over it.   (*Francis Coomber*)

Shrubsole who was Maidstone mayor in 1935 and Emmy acted as his mayoress and enjoyed the experience greatly. Other members of the family lived in Tyland Lane and inspired the name Shrubsole Drive. Emmy was very active in the social club and most other local affairs.

Amongst all these houses was a very tiny general shop run by Bill Longley and his wife, they living in the bungalow alongside it. Elsie Muffett remembers the shop being so small that Mrs Longley could remain seated and still reach around for almost any required item. She kept several nanny goats tethered outside, presumably for their milk. Parafin was one item sold, and Mrs Nissen remembers the smell of it pervading the little building. It was Bill Longley's kind nature to serve anyone anytime. Local miscreants would watch for the bungalow lights to go out signifying Bill's bedtime, and then knock him up to buy some roll-your-own cigarette papers. In time the little shop was demolished when a good-sized store was built on the corner with Tyland Lane, run at one time by Ernie and Ethel Spoff.

Come the 1930s and across the road and up towards Tyland Farm there were built the distinctive semi-detached houses known unsurprisingly as "the green tops". They were set well back, perhaps with future road widening in mind. In their early days the run of green tops was known as the Cobtree Estate.

The "green tops" in 2012.

The Lodge in 2012.

CHAPTER 6

Life at the Chatham Road Lodge

We drop back down the Chatham Road to the Lodge which we passed by in the last chapter. Ernie Gates had arrived in 1932 to work for Garrard at the zoo, and he and his wife Rosa lived in the Lodge. He was known to all and sundry as Captain Gates and although he served in the First War dealing with cavalry horses it is doubtful that he held a commission. Was it bestowed upon him by Garrard for some reason? Was it a circus term? Nobody seems to know.

Mrs Gates died around 1939 and Ernie felt the need to have a housekeeper. There then appeared upon Sandling's stage a lady to whom adjectives such as exotic, romantic, mysterious, kind, friendly and more besides might apply. Ernie's housekeeper was Netta (short for Henrietta) Jarmann and close by is a picture of her when young. She was olive-skinned, had jet black hair, and wore long ear-rings. Local people tried to guess her background. Was she Italian or Spanish or Hungarian or from some other East European country? People thought that she spoke with a slight accent and as an example she addressed Dinah Reid as "Deena". She was very well-spoken.

Her son Danny tells that she was in fact born in England, later marrying a policeman. To Danny's ear there

Netta Jarmann in 1928.
(Danny Jarmann)

was no foreign accent, but he does confirm that Netta probably took delight in confusing people and telling a tale of two. For example, she told of having been married to a Spanish bull-fighter, and of coming from a family who once owned even more land than the Cobtree estate, and having been a model for Vogue. Danny can at least confirm that she had done some modelling.

The Lodge when Netta arrived in 1940 with baby Danny was basic in the extreme, with no gas or electricity and relying upon paraffin for heating and candles for light. For a long time there was no piped water, just a well outside from which Jim Murray ran a lead pipe to the sink. Danny used to stand on a box and pump up what was required. Later on George Brundle, who was grazing cows nearby, installed a water trough for the animals and kindly ran a pipe off it to the Lodge. It was not buried very deep and would freeze in the winter. At times Netta would collect ice from the pond and melt it in a saucepan.

There was an outside toilet which you flushed using a bucket dipped into a rainwater barrel. Cooking was on a range fired by coal or wood, and Danny would earn pocket money from Ernie for collecting wood where he could. Anything approaching a proper wash was in a tin bath. Netta would curtain if off with a clothes horse draped in towels for some degree of privacy. Ernie Gates would get in first, then Netta, and Danny last of all in water which had become rather murky.

The pond was close by the Lodge where there were dozens of ducks. Danny tells of her saying to them "Are you coming?" whereupon they would all waddle after her indoors to be fed in comfort. The ducks would keep them well supplied with eggs, and then some would end up on the dining table.

With a hint of the gypsy about her, Netta would tell fortunes, grabbing hands or more often swirling tea leaves around in the bottom of a cup. If it was for a youngster she would say "You must never thank me". She would turn up at local fetes to tell fortunes, but one day foresaw somebody drowning and after that did it no more.

She was extremely fond of children, and when she heard of a new arrival she would call with a little present, usually something that she had knitted. Linda Ellis was one recipient, a soft toy with long bandy legs. Linda recalls her "brushing away thanks with her lovely smile". For adults moving into the locality she would quietly leave tea and biscuits on their doorsteps.

Sadly Netta grew old. Captain Gates had died in 1963. Both Linda Ellis and Margaret Dracup remember her struggling to cross what had become a dual carriageway, hauling her shopping trolley. Moving as fast as her elderly legs could carry her. Margaret would sometimes help with her shopping. "Coopers marmalade please. And course-cut mind". Netta loved to eat a pigeon, which she would make last two days.

She had become rather deaf (for a reason to be told in a later chapter) and this began to make it difficult for some people to converse with her. In the Tyland Lane corner shop some assistants would see her coming and disappear, leaving Elsie Muffett to serve her. To Elsie she was "a lovely old lady". Despite her deafness she was always aware when Peter Kirby pushed at the creaky iron gates on his way for some unauthorised fishing. She would insist on him coming in for a chat. She was never employed by Garrard, and Peter's naughty intentions were of no concern to her.

And what of Ernie Gates himself? To Danny as he was growing up he was a father figure, teaching him how to snare rabbits and other country skills. Giving him the tip to only take two eggs from a moorhen's nest, leave the rest, and the hen would continue laying. Ernie would buy a piglet at Maidstone market and fatten it for Christmas. Danny helped to remove the bristles from the dead pig's skin, keeping a supply of hot water to soften them. In contrast, Ernie would bring home any sick animals from the zoo and Netta would help nurse them back to health. Even a sheep on one occasion.

At the time of writing, the Lodge still stands but in a ruinous state and marooned with busy roads surrounding it. Linda Ellis tells that Netta had an accident with a candle and was moved to a Home, dying at the age of 85. Upon washing her hair, nurses found that it was genuinely still jet black, putting paid to rumours that she might have used shoe polish! Danny feels that with her colouring she must have had some ancestry rooted in sunny climes. What a wonderful character. The nearby golf course remembers her with a hole named "Jarmann's Drive".

The Lodge can next lead us into memories of the zoo itself.

Ernie "Captain" Gates.   *(Danny Jarmann)*

Netta and Danny. Circa 1948.   *(Danny Jarmann)*

Sir Garrard Tyrwhitt-Drake. (*Bob Corner*)

CHAPTER 7

The Zoo

The zoo's official title was Maidstone Zoo, and Vickie Harris's book does it the fullest justice in telling its story. In a brief and necessary summary, Garrard's private collection of animals had grown since the First War and in 1934 he opened his zoo to the public. He himself recalled that an estimated eight thousand five hundred people "besieged the gates and were held up in huge queues".

Dinah Reid provides the following memories. In 1939 at the age of fourteen she left school and got a job at the zoo. She lived with her parents in Gillingham, and as she could not afford the bus fare she used to cycle all the way to Cobtree, and then struggle back home via long and steep Bluebell Hill. But the hill was a delight on the way to work, whizzing all the way down and often sailing past the zoo entrance with screeching brakes and breathing in the lovely aromas coming from the Garden Bakery.

Dinah's job was to look after the baby animals, especially those in Pets Corner. She remembers a cage with two monkeys whom she would greet each morning with "Hello Louis, hello Jane". Winters could be very cold, and she would wear pyjamas under her jodhpurs. Garrard would not allow skirts, and called the girls as well as the men staff by their surnames. Lady Edna, whom they all addressed as Madam, did call the girls by their Christian names. Garrard would try and find time to make an inspection of all the animals every day.

At Christmas dressed birds were laid out for the staff to choose to take home. But Garrard standing by would say "Not that big turkey, that's mine". The girls also got some expensive soap, nicely boxed and ribboned.

One day after cleaning out the lion's cage the keeper forgot to pull down the shutter grill as he left. Both lion and lioness walked free and there was panic. Garrard summoned the Army with instructions to shoot if necessary. Somehow the lioness was tempted into the public toilets and re-captured, but the lion did have to be shot.

The lions in particular

consumed much meat. John Allison heard tell of old London horses no longer fit for work being transported in cattle trucks and unloaded at Aylesford station. Then the poor old things were led at a pathetically slow pace along Forstal Road to Cobtree where they were to be slaughtered.

Around 1954 some wolves escaped. There was a wolf wood enclosed by a high fence. It had snowed heavily and one section of fencing collapsed and the snow built up to form a ramp over which the wolves climbed. Words of alarm were spread and the police went around warning people. Alan Veitch at Cossington Farm heard the news and thought it wise to have his shotgun with him. Alan, reckoned one of the best shots in the district, spotted one wolf and killed it. Another wolf is thought to have been shot as well, and certainly Brenda Steadman remembers seeing the dead body of a large wolf whose tracks in the snow were followed by keepers. Alan Veitch at neighbouring Cossington was well placed for exciting events, and remembers a kangaroo escaping. Another time he retrieved a peacock with some effort, returned it to Garrard, and merely received a glass of lemonade for his trouble.

The most exciting and also dangerous event was in 1952 when Daisy the elephant, apparently frightened by a jet aircraft flying overhead, ran off in panic and collapsed on the ground. Nothing would encourage or persuade Daisy to get up, not even one person's suggestion of prodding her hard with a six inch nail. Garrard arrived on the

Elsie and Doris Waters bestowing their stage names of Gert and Daisy upon two elephants. *(Vickie Harris)*

scene and help was summoned from all directions, including Bob Corner and his dad from Tyland Farm. Bob tells the story.

A tractor was brought over and block and tackle hooked over a sturdy tree branch. A circus was performing some distance away and Garrard requested their expert help. Some thirteen people were assembled and after five or six hours of great effort Daisy was at last winched to her feet. But worse was to follow. Once on her feet Daisy ran amok, charging everyone in sight. People fled for safety in all directions, none moving faster than Garrard himself.

With great reluctance Garrard felt that the only solution now was to shoot poor Daisy. He called upon Bob's father to do the deed, but Bill Corner protested that he was too old and shaky, and proposed Bob for the job. Now to kill an elephant weighing several tons called for very special cartridges, supplied by Sanders in Maidstone at some cost. Garrard told Bob to aim not between the eyes but behind the shoulder, and that as the cartridges were expensive to make sure he used only one. With Bob poised to shoot, a miracle occurred. Daisy calmed down completely and allowed herself to be led away. The elephant boy later found signs of a decayed tooth which led to speculation that this might have been another cause of Daisy's distress.

Not quite so dramatic was when another elephant wandered off into the clay pit used by brick manufacturers off Pratling Street. The creature got stuck and another elephant was brought to haul it out. When yet another elephant named Lillie who came from a circus eventually died she was without any ceremony buried in the dung heap behind the elephant house.

At some point in time it seems that Garrard kept the elephants shackled, but when a new keeper arrived he was against this. He was a German named Karl Fischer (known as Ponk) who would let them loose for exercise, and play some form of hide and seek with them. Presumably it was Ponk who did the hiding! Hopefully the elephants also enjoyed having howdahs on their backs for visitors to have rides. And hopefully an elephant called Sally enjoyed her naming ceremony performed by Gracie Fields in 1938, in the course of which the famous singer entertained an estimated ten thousand visitors with a rendition of her hit song "Sally". Stuart Murray remembers Ponk washing the elephants in the lake and using a broom as a scrubbing brush.

Vickie Harris in her book tells of other escaping animals, including a bear and a camel. And that over the years the staff endured a few nips and bites. Vickie also tells that during the war an unwanted parrot was taken in. "The bird was an excellent talker, but unfortunately it must have spent its formative years in bad company, for its language consisted almost exclusively of oaths and obscenities, so much so that there were complaints from visitors".

It is thought to be Vickie who told of how Karl Fischer persuaded Garrard that the elephants just loved biscuits. Garrard's heart was softened and he gave Karl a continuous supply, which Karl and an accomplice happily consumed themselves.

One thing that people remember even above the animals was the little train that

Garrard with two elephants wearing shackles.

could transport people for several hundred yards from the Chatham Road entrance to the ticket office. Malcolm Shelmerdine has recorded some very useful information about it. The track he thought was probably once used in some local quarry, and the locomotive was certainly ex-quarry. It was a single track with the engine "pulling out and pushing back". It was all set up in 1937 and the engine was named "Jessie" in a ceremony performed by the actress Jessie Matthews. The up fare for adults was two pence, and down one penny, with children half price. But Brenda Steadman's parents said that she could only go one way as it was costly!

The zoo closed in 1959, and when Garrard died five years later that marked another closure to a particularly colourful period in the life of Sandling and the wider life of Maidstone.

A Zoo train.   *(Mary Thomas)*

The Butchery at Cobtree

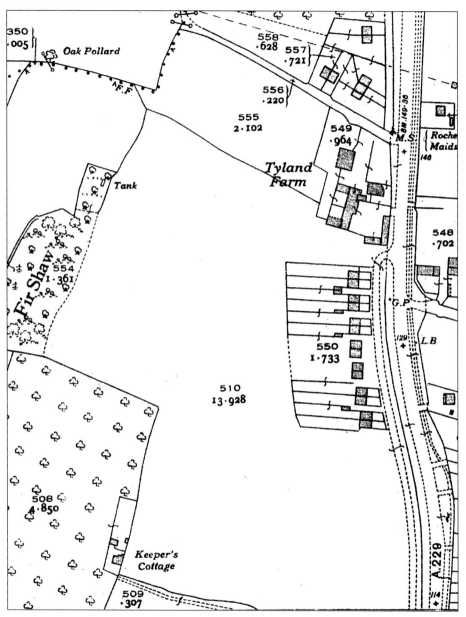

1938 and the first green tops have just been built. Keeper's Cottage bottom left.

CHAPTER 8

Tyland Farm

It will be remembered from chapter 2 that George Brundle had been taken on by Garrard in 1925 to run both Sandling and Tyland Farms, and that soon afterwards Bill Corner arrived to help him. Bill came from a family of thatchers in Suffolk. He always built his hay and corn stacks round, and Wally Bishop would joke that he didn't like corners. Bill lived at Keeper's Cottage, due west of where the green tops were later to be built. Access was by a long track which emerged onto the Chatham Road alongside the most southern of the run of green tops.

Keeper's Cottage was very basic, with an outside toilet and no gas, electricity or water. There was a well with a pump, but unpleasant leeches tended to come up with the water. Rather better was a dip hole near the well fed by spring water which was fit for drinking after being boiled. Lighting was by oil lamps. When the green tops were built Bill arranged with Garrard for a proper water supply to be provided, and he and fellow workers dug an extremely long trench for pipework to be laid up to Chatham Road and connect to the water main there.

Behind Keeper's Cottage was an orchard from which the family had pickings, though most was gathered for sale by Garrard. Later six breeding sows were kept in the orchard, whilst Bill's wife had up to a hundred chicken.

At Keeper's Cottage in 1930 was born Bob Corner, and it is his memories which feed this chapter. He left school at fourteen and after an apprenticeship with Drake & Fletcher qualified as an agricultural engineer. He was then employed by both farms, working closely with his father. In 1951 Bob married June, and there follows in his own words an account of their wedding, and tells of a different and far simpler world:

Our Wedding Day
22nd September 1951

"June and I met at Drake & Fletcher's Social Club, playing table tennis. I lived at Sandling and worked at Tyland Farm and June lived in Maidstone and worked at Highfield's children's nursery, London Road, Maidstone. The average wage was between £4 and £6 per week. We were married at Boxley Church on 22nd September at 2pm by the Reverend Mortimer Lamb. Hardly anyone had cars in those days as they were still in short supply and most of the cars were pre-war vintage. Petrol was still rationed and cost 1/5d per gallon (7p). June was driven to church in my father's car, a 1938 Vauxhall 10. The bridesmaids were taken to church by my brother-in-law Don in his car. The reception was held at Sandling Social Club and the hire charge was 3/- an hour (15p), including gas.

Clothes were still rationed so June borrowed a wedding dress, and I had a suit made to measure at Fifty Shilling Tailors in Maidstone with my clothing coupons. It cost about £3, June's bouquet was red carnations and the bridesmaids had small baskets of mixed flowers.

Because Boxley was remote and there was no bus service, we hired a coach from Maidstone and District Bus Company. We managed to arrange for this to be driven by Cecil Kitney, a Brother-in-Law of my uncle. He also had a band, and this ensured he would be available to play at the reception in the evening. The coach picked our guests up from Maidstone and went to Boxley via Sandling, and returned to Sandling Social Club after the ceremony. As far as I can remember this cost about £3. When we left the church we drove all around the village (it was a small community then) and everyone came out and waved.

Food was still rationed but June's mother managed to arrange for a caterer in Week Street to do the catering. He managed to get some extra food coupons and we had a reasonable spread. Sherry was difficult to obtain, but when we mentioned Sir Garrard and Lady Tyrwhitt-Drake (Mayor and Mayoress of Maidstone) would be guests, he managed to get a better quality and a sweet, medium and dry. About 50 guests came and we had a three tier wedding cake. After the wedding my father lent us his car for a week and we went to Suffolk for our honeymoon to stay with two elderly aunts Alice and Florrie.

After we were married we went to live at Tyland Farm. We had no bathroom or inside toilet – just an outside toilet in a shed at the top of the garden. The only heating was by coal fires. The kitchen had a cold water tap over a brown sink and a big stone copper for washing clothes in the corner. We had electric lighting and two electric sockets but if we tried to use both of them

Tyland Farmhouse before restoration.   *(Bob Corner)*

the lights went out. Eventually we turned the pantry into a bathroom. The bath was rescued from the fields where it had been used as a drinking trough for the cows but we gave it a good wash before using. The hot water tank was the old storage tank for the automatic drinking bowls in the cowshed but to us at the time it was a taste of luxury.

At that time the main Maidstone to Chatham Road was close to Tyland Farm and our bedroom faced the road. Out best man and great friend Sid Welfare commuted to Dartford and was on the first bus every morning at 5.30am. Most mornings the bus had the same driver and Sid persuaded him to sound the horn and the passengers to shout "wakey wakey" every morning. This carried on for several weeks."

As the account mentions, Bob and June made Tyland Farmhouse their home. The building is dated late 1500s to early 1600s with the western end possibly having been added in the mid 1850s. Bob's account shows how basic it was.

Tyland Farm was mostly arable, and with cattle grazing on the grassland. George Brundle concentrated on the cows and did the milking at Sandling Farm. With each cow taking ten to fifteen minutes to milk it was labour intensive. At one time Bob's mother had a spell of getting up at five-thirty in the morning and walking the half mile from Keeper's Cottage to help with the milking. And then sometimes again in the afternoon. George Brundle said that she had a way of getting the cows to relax and was one of the best milkers he had ever seen.

In the early days there was no tractor and all the work was done by horses. Sandling Farm was fairly easy as it was sandy with very few stones. But at Tyland the soil was much heavier and stonier, and patches of gault clay did not help. The going was so difficult that they used to plough downhill and return "empty" – that is with the plough blades raised, and then re-start from uphill.

A corn stack behind Tyland Barn.
Charlie Russell on the ladder.
(Bob Corner)

A lot of damage was caused by the high rabbit population, many living amongst brambles in an old sandpit. Behind Stream Cottages in Forstal Road was a large meadow known as the Warren, and in the middle was a massive rabbit burrow. Local policeman Ted Kirby kept ferrets, as did Tommy Vincent who worked at Cossington Farm. Bill Corner joined them and told how the three took over two hours to set the nets, put in twenty-seven ferrets and caught over one hundred rabbits. After this success Garrard and his wife gave permission for Bill to both shoot and ferret in the disused sandpit.

As related in the Sandling Farm chapter, George Brundle's father had helped him financially for two years. When things got very difficult in the 1930s George and Bill Corner sought further help, but were told that they must now stand on their own feet. It seems that on a few occasions Bill paid the men's wages out of his own pocket. He was probably able to do this because the breeding sows in his orchard and his wife's chicken were both earning them money.

50

Bill Corner on farmland which is now lost to roads. Above, behind Bakery Cottages. Below, behind Tyland Barn. *(Bob Corner)*

George Brundle retired in 1980. The coming of the new line of the A229 in its various stages, coupled with the M20 and its slip roads, took much of the farmland. New arrivals to the Bluebell Estate in 1988 found Tyland Barn standing vacant, but Bob and June Corner continued living in the farmhouse until 1997. Doug Poole recalls that there had been a plan to dismantle the barn and re-erect it at the Kent Life Museum. Individual bricks were numbered to assist the re-build. Developers no doubt had their eyes on the site, as did the Village Hall committee when a new hall was being considered. Then the Kent Wildlife Trust acquired the site, renovating both barn and farmhouse to very high standards, preserving an important part of Sandling's history.

The Barn in course of restoration 1991. (Alan Moultrie)

In 2012 Bob Corner and Wally Bishop pay a nostalgic visit to a restored Tyland Farmhouse.

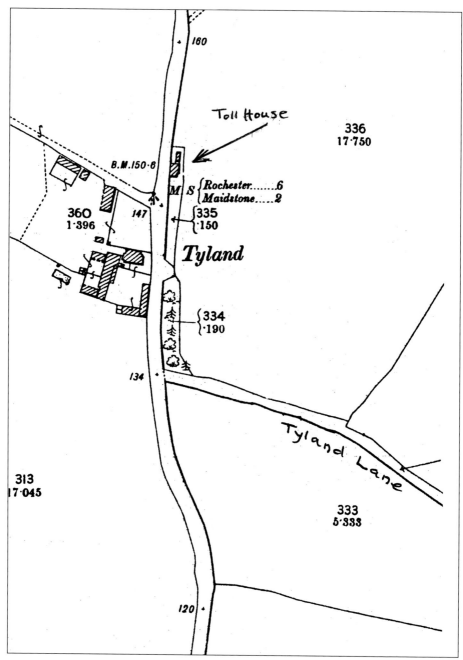

1897

CHAPTER 9

The Tollhouse

The 1897 map bestows the name "Tyland" to the area which it shows. Tyland Farm has pride of place with its old farmhouse and barns, and over the road we see the building which was the old Tollhouse. See how it is sited right close to the road, the idea being that those needing to pay a toll could hand their coins in through the window. Turnpikes arose in the 1700s, were not surprisingly unpopular, and around 1869 were phased out. How much you paid depended upon what kind of wagon or cart, how many horses, what manner of livestock.

This was an old Roman road, and one used for centuries. We might pause to consider all manner of people and traffic who have passed up and down. From Roman soldiers to the earliest motor cars; galloping horses; stage coaches and trudging peasants. Sir Thomas Wyatt leading his rebels towards Rochester. Possibly even King Harold hurrying down to Hastings?

Bob Beeby understood that the road was widened in 1932, in the course of which the old Tollhouse was demolished, and new Tollhouse Cottage stands in its place, set much further back.

Once the road had been widened people began to refer to it as the concrete road. Further road works took place over the years, and Bob Beeby told of a mysterious tunnel being discovered close by Tyland Barn, one that you could walk through. Then when the dual carriageway was being constructed Peter Kirby remembers a lined tunnel being discovered, though this one you had to stoop to pass along. Bob thought that the tunnel he heard of may have connected with Cossington Farm, run in later years by the Veitch family. On the 1897 map, the track leading west above the Tyland Farm buildings became known as Veitch's Track or Lane.

Those two tunnels remain a mystery. Peter Kirby remembers that in dry weather the parched earth used to reveal a diagonal line from Tyland Meadow (close by Tollhouse Cottage) running towards Boarley farmhouse. Was this some connection?

The Tollhouse was adjacent to the land of Boarley Farm and some of their labourers occupied it. Indeed, Bob Beeby and his new wife lived there for a while when first married. In 1942 Jim Dowle's grandmother Mrs Ashdown was living there and Stuart Murray was impressed that Jessie Dowle used to walk all the way from Grange Farm over Boxley Hill to visit her mum. Ironically, in his young days Stuart himself got work at Grange Farm and walked there all the way from Sandling, via Tyland Lane, Boarley Lane, Pilgrims Way then all the way up Boxley Hill to the farm. And walk back home at day's end. How people walked in those days.

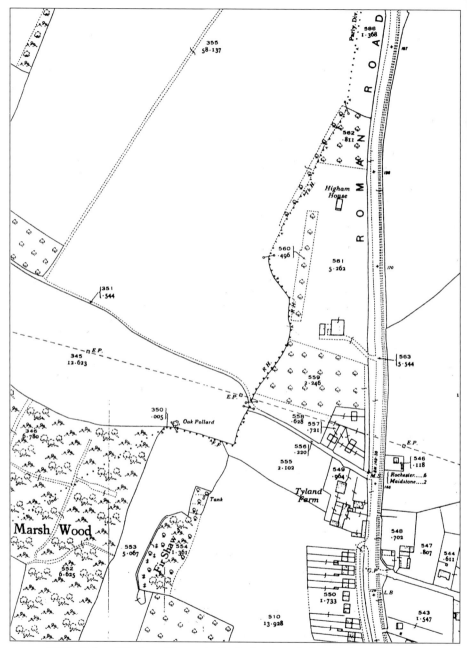

1938. Below Higham House is the bakery, and then Bakery Cottages.

CHAPTER 10

The Garden Bakery

Around 1936 there arrived in Sandling Mr Frederick Albert Smith. He was an established baker and came from Tonbridge. The 1938 map helps to explain what he created. He built a splendid new state of the art bakery to the north of Tyland Farm, built for himself an attractive home Higham House, and built for his workers a group of seven houses which are still known as Bakery Cottages. These houses became known as the Garden Bakery Estate, though to others less glamorously as Smith's Estate.

Brenda Steadman (nee Bathurst) and her brother Tony have many memories, as their father Les worked at the bakery, and the family lived in one of the Bakery Cottages. Les was a renowned baker and was known as "doughnut" or "doughie". All manner of wedding, celebration and other cakes were produced. Fred Smith's land included orchards of cherries, plums and greengages, and two odd-job boys would pick the fruit and keep everything tidy. Mr Smith would walk to the bakery from Higham House through an avenue of pear trees.

Mr Smith maintained a whole fleet of vans to make deliveries, and at one time drove himself around in what was to John Bradford from Tyland Lane "an enviable Bristol car". There was a tennis court at Higham House which on one occasion Mrs Smith had cut and marked out for John and a friend to play, but payment of sixpence was requested.

It must have been the mid 1950s when Mr Smith retired and the bakery closed down. Other businesses came to use the building and then moved on, the best known being

Mr. Smith with his wife, young son and Bakery staff. *(Brenda Steadman)*

OAKHIVE
The store where
service and
savings meet

Always a superb selection
of Electrical Appliances,
Audio, TV, Kitchens, Carpets,
Furniture & Jewellery

🏠**Oakhive**

☆ where service and savings meet ☆
Oakvale House, Chatham Road, Maidstone.
Telephone: Maidstone 65454

Higham House.   *(The Lane family)*

Harrisons the seed merchants from Maidstone. Brenda worked for them for a while, and had a lovely walk to work from Bakery Cottages through the orchards. The final business to move in was Oakhive, an early out of town store selling mostly white electrical goods.

Into the 1980s and Oakhive moved out and the land was acquired by developers who in due time built the houses of the Bluebell Estate. Ian and Sue Flockhart were the first purchasers to move in, and no sooner had they arrived than they received a letter about the proposed High Speed Rail route, which in their case was planned to pass right through their house. Other new arrivals had the same welcoming letter. This resulted in a severe "blight" on the estate and it is understood that out of some sixty-two houses only three families stayed put, whilst the rest sold to the railway company and moved out. The blight continued for some time and the railway, being unable to find people brave enough to buy, rented out those houses they had acquired. Things did, of course, settle down eventually. But attractive Higham House came to be destroyed by fire and more houses built upon its site.

Opposite Tollgate Way there was for some years after the Second War a cricket ground, on land which was part of Boarley Farm. Bob Beeby's father made the land available and a Tyland Cricket Club was formed and played there for some years, not too many of the players being local men. The Club packing up co-incided with Drake & Fletcher having lost their own ground to still more road works around Maidstone. Jack Rumble's job interview with Geoffrey Fletcher somehow saw the subject arise, and the Beebys were more than happy to accommodate Drake & Fletcher who continued to use the ground until about 1970. Geoffrey was captain and a very keen cricketer. On the cricket field his employees were encouraged to call him by his Christian name and forget that he was their boss. And if he dropped a catch ....

Peter Kirby remembers the ground with its pavilion and trees around. Drake & Fletcher looked after it all, and had a special gala weekend in the summer. Mr Smith

The author and other young cricketers from Barming arrive to play Tyland C.C. in 1957.

also held a fete there for his staff. Les Bathurst used to love going across to sit and watch the cricket and as head of his household insisted upon a cup of tea being brought over, rather than taking a flask with him. Today, all that remains is one old oak tree standing as a sad sentinel.

Tony Bathurst and sister Brenda remember how busy the Chatham Road was around 1950 and how difficult it could be to cross. From upstairs in their house they could see the bus they needed for school coming down Bluebell Hill and have time to get to the stop near Tyland Farm. Some years before this Stuart Murray remembers open-top buses which had leather covers to pull over at least your knees if it rained. In snowy weather it was cinders rather than salt which was thrown down. If you were so inclined, you could walk from Maidstone to Chatham on pavements. If you looked back towards Sandling from near the Lower Bell you would see cattle and sheep grazing, pigs and chicken in fields, hop gardens and orchards.

Arthur Whale in charge of a game at one of many fetes at Tyland.
(Margaret McCarthy)

58

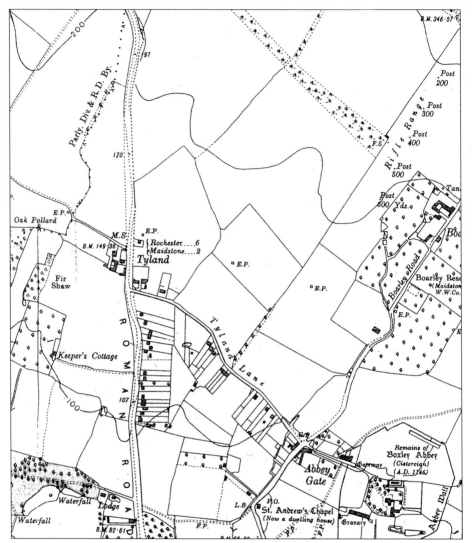

In 1931 the houses in Tyland Lane have begun to be built, but no green tops yet, and no Garden Bakery.

CHAPTER 11

Tyland Lane

Because the modern A229 dual carriageway is sited to the west of Tyland Barn and the green tops, a stretch of the Old Chatham Road survives in relative calm. You can cross the road in comfort from Tyland Barn and begin a walk down Tyland Lane.

The western end is the only part of the lane which has buildings on its north side, and most are there through connections with Boarley Farm. To them this corner of their farmland was Tyland Farm, in disregard of the confusion this might cause with the much older Tyland Farm across the Chatham Road. The long barn building survives as part of the Tyland Corner cluster of business units. Peter Kirby became very familiar with the long barn, which he describes as the main meeting place for local youths in his own young days, and it had an upper floor. Here was much fun and games. During the summer Bob Beeby allowed the Church to hold a jumble sale there. Between the barn and its surrounds, and the cricket field higher up, was Tyland Meadow. Here cows used to graze all the year round, and in early summer Peter remembers it having a yellow carpet of buttercups from one side to the other. From time to time Bob Beeby would allow the meadow to be used for fetes by local organisations, and it was yet another playground for youngsters.

Tom Rumble
(Jack Rumble)

The first property down on the left is what was built in 1956 as a police house. Ted Kirby had retired as the local policeman in 1944 and he was succeeded by Tom Rumble who had been assisting him during the difficult war years. Tom had his own house "Rosedale" in Tyland Lane but was required to move into the new police house when it was ready, renting out his own. His area was from Aylesford Forstal across to Weavering, and from Penenden Heath up to Cossington in one direction, and up to Harp Farm over the hill in another. This large area he covered on his bicycle. Brenda Steadman called for this assistance once and Tom replied – "Hang on. I'll pump my tyres up and get my boots on". According to son Jack he was forever pumping his tyres up and brushing his clothes down. He sat very upright on his bike and gave very precise hand signals if he was directing traffic. Peter Kirby once found a ten shilling note in Tyland Lane and handed it in at the police house. Tom took an age noting details down and getting the record right. Being unclaimed after the prescribed length of time, the note was duly presented to Peter.

As we saw in Chapter 1, Tom spent hours directing traffic by The Running Horse, sometimes until 10pm. Boys escaping from Borstal would often make for the Downs to hide for awhile, and Tom was the one asked to look out for them. He re-captured most, but was annoyed when one escaped. But he felt better when told that the lad was something of a champion runner.

Some of Tom's duties involved the farming community, as son Jack remembers. Tom would spend nearly all day supervising sheep dipping for the Beebys in Boarley Lane, their dip being just before the oast. There he would smoke his pipe and drink large amounts of tea. Around Christmas one year poachers were stealing chicken, and Tom and his sergeant spent a whole night in huts on Mr Hamilton's Abbey Farm to keep a lookout. Tom was very good when dealing with gypsies and persuading them to move on. This was the case in the 1960s when quite a large gypsy camp was set up between The Yew Tree and Lower Grange Farm. Tom was a dab hand at first aid, and it is said that at least once he acted as a midwife.

Stuart Murray was unlucky enough to be hit by foot and mouth disease in 1952, affecting his cows, pigs and sheep. Tom Rumble was assigned the task of controlling visitors so that the disease did not spread. Tom actually slept at the Murrays' house "Rochester Meadow" for two or three nights. After slaughter, the corpses were burnt and then buried. Pat Sandford remembers seeing the flames from his lime works on Bluebell Hill.

Tom retired in about 1966, and the police house was sold into private hands. Jeff and Jennifer Friend became owners and they inherited a very unusual feature. Tucked away was a nuclear alarm. A covenant on the deeds required them to always have their phone in working order and to co-operate with the authorities. They were even supplied with a geiger counter and maroons to fire off if appropriate. One day the alarm went off and Jeff rang the police for instructions but they knew nothing. It transpired that an inquisitive girl in an office somewhere had asked herself – "I wonder what that button's for?" she pressed it and several nuclear alarms around Maidstone screamed their false warning.

Next to the old police house are numbers 1, 2 and 3 Tyland Cottages which were created out of what was once a single farmhouse for this corner of Boarley Farm. From this point on, along the north side of the lane is agricultural land.

We turn to the south side, and it is worth referring to the Abbey Court map of 1891 in chapter 4, when Tyland Lane was a simple track way with no buildings whatsoever. Houses began to be built on the south side in the 1920s, and the 1931 map shows what had been built by then. Other houses were to follow, including those down Shrubsole Drive and Shenley Grove. About halfway along, an access way led down to what became known as Willow Industries (or even just "the industries"). This has always been the location for business activities of many kinds. Particularly well-remembered is Miss Margaret Jenner who ran a small plant nursery which included greenhouses. Local boy Jack Rumble remembers helping out, wrapping up bundles of plants in newspaper secured by a rubber band, after which Miss Jenner would set off on her bicycle to make deliveries. The sight of her cycling purposefully around is in many people's memories. She lived with her mother who was very house proud and would not allow the bike in the house. Upon mum's death Margaret did what she had always wanted to do and parked her bike indoors. Others recall different forms of transport, even a three-wheeled motor-bike and trailer.

Peter Kirby lived in Shrubsole Drive and his mother used to help at the nursery picking beans and vegetables. Peter remembers Miss Jenner as a wonderful person. As well as plants and vegetables she kept pigs. Not far away at Tyland Farm Bill Corner had a pedigree boar to service his sows, going by the name of King David. Now and again King David would make his escape and trot down Tyland Lane and pay a romantic visit to Miss Jenner's sows. Bob Corner remembers Miss Jenner as a "down to earth farmer". Her family owned a lot of land, with some fronting to Boarley Lane on which they had a bungalow built.

Another prominent figure at the Industries was Bob Stoneham who had a slaughterhouse there (which is where King David ended up) and a butcher's shop. During the war, when the Government was anxious to see food and ingredients eked out to best advantage, he was prosecuted because his sausages contained too much meat. He is also remembered as a cattle dealer, and it was he who had Willow Farmhouse built, and he was behind building some of the later houses in the lane. And as if these activities were not enough he also came to run a bakery, with a shop at Penenden Heath.

Living on the corner of Shenley Grove was Jack Bradford who with his wife had worked extremely hard to lay the foundations of their fishmonger business which found its final and successful home in Earl Street, Maidstone. Jack never forgot his own hard times and would frequently help others in need. One now very prominent firm told Jack in later years that without his generosity they might never have become so successful. His son John remembers how few cars there were along Tyland Lane in the 1950s. He and Doug Pocock would mark out their cricket pitch in the lane using two apple boxes and very rarely be disturbed. Eileen Hook has exactly the same memory. And then again, Peter Kirby paints a similar picture. On one occasion he helped to make a cart on wheels using an old wardrobe as the main body, strings to pull and steer, and spy holes drilled for the driver to hopefully see where he was going. The first lad to try out this "mobile coffin" was given a push and made his uncontrolled way along the lane and crashed into the wall of Abbey Gate farmhouse.

Halfway along the north side of the lane and dividing the agricultural land is a narrow strip of woodland known as Deadman's Shaw. Betty Kirby always said it was so named because a tramp had fallen into his fire there and died. Others say that the tramp or somebody else hung themselves from a tree. On a dark and windy night, when the boughs are creaking, many people have found it scary having to pass by the spot.

A stream coming from Boarley crosses under Tyland Lane at its eastern end, giving to a home there the name Bridgewater. For very many years there were hop gardens along Tyland Lane, and these require a chapter of their own, which follows.

The end of Tyland Lane used to flood when the culvert carrying the stream could not cope.
Circa 1962.   *(The Beeby family)*

Two hopping scenes in Tyland Lane circa 1907. (Rev. Hilton / Ruth Saveall)

CHAPTER 12

The Hop Gardens

Elsie Parrett remembers the hop picking at Tyland Lane and Boarley before the Second War, when Bob Style was the landowner. George and Charlie Brooker were still the tenants, but it seems that Bob Style was retaining for his own use the hops and fruit. That arrangement presumably changed when the Beebys arrived in the late 1930s. Bob Style would put in an appearance now and again, and when the season's picking was done he would arrange for a hop trailer to appear with small red apples for the pickers to tuck into. Elsie remembers Mr Saveall from Boxley village being the booky, whom she found rather stern and strict.

Most people's memories are of the post-war years. Along Tyland Lane there were several gaps in the hedges to allow the pickers access. Local people would make their way on foot, people from Maidstone or Chatham might use the regular buses which stopped near Tyland Barn, whilst at times Dennis Beeby or one of the farm workers would take a vehicle to collect pickers from places such as Ringlestone, Robin Hood Lane and Walderslade. There was never any shortage of such pickers.

Peter Kirby's memories feed much of this chapter, and he tells of three distinct hop gardens which he knew as follows. One was Tyland Hops opposite where he lived in Shrubsole Drive, and then Shenley Hops opposite Shenley Grove. The third was on the corner of Tyland Lane and Boarley Lane which he knew as Robboe's Hops because of the Robinson family living on the opposite corner. Boarley Farm also had a fourth hop garden known as Bushy field sited north-east of the Abbey.

In 1944 a sixteen years old Pat Sandford got a job at Boarley Farm, being set at that time upon a farming career. In charge of the hop gardens as foreman measurer was Eileen Hook's dad Fred

Fred Excell in the hop-picking shed.
(Eileen Hook)

64

Excell, and Pat having gone to Grammar school Fred thought him well suited to be his booker. Pat would trot behind Fred as bins were checked and measured. Fred would frequently find faults, which caused mutterings and threats of mutiny from the Ringlestone ladies in particular. But you didn't argue with Fred. When it was time to stop you stopped, because Fred's stentorian voice would shout "Pull no more bines"!

Tony Bathhurst remembers when young having to fill an open umbrella with hops before being allowed to disappear and play in Deadman's Shaw. Sister Brenda was told off for picking too many leaves and was excused doing any more picking at all. John Bradford would nip across to pick hops just for the fun of it. Other lads would take pickings from other people's bins and transfer them to their own, or to their mother's, sometimes creeping over at night when all was quiet. John remembers Fred Excell being puzzled how some of the boys had managed to pick so much. Haydn Beeby so enjoyed the fun of it all that he got more than usually annoyed at having to start a new term at school with hopping still in full swing.

Certainly in the 1930s if not later, some ladies (out for the fresh air and not wishing to be thought in need of extra money) would pick into what was variously called the charity bin or hospital bin. The money earnt would then go to a good cause. It is said that the regular pickers would make sure that these bins were located in some distant shady corner. Though converted now to dwellings, the structure of the three kiln oasthouse still stands in Boarley Lane as a reminder of those hopping days. There was

Hops growing close by the oast   *(Eileen Hook)*

Hops being hoisted up to the drying floor.
(The Beeby family).

And below, inside the drying floor.
(Eileen Hook)

always a rush to finish the August harvesting because the oast was used to dry grain, and needed to be clear and ready for September's hops which were transported there for drying. Men would stay in the oast all night to keep the fires going and it became very hot. Jack Rumble would help and was allowed to sleep in there on one occasion. So too Tony Bathhurst and pals, using hop pockets for sleeping bags. The fire embers were ideal for baking potatoes. When Peter Kirby helped out in the oast he found the smells magical.

When drying was complete, all these willing hands would shovel the hops into hop pockets. These were pressed tight, stitched up and stencilled with Boarley Farm's business name of Saywell and Beeby. Fred Excell and Dennis Beeby were in the thick of all this action, after which the filled pockets were transported away. Then fresh picking arrived and the whole process would be repeated over several weeks until there were no more bines left to pull. Pay day was an obvious highlight, and pickers would gather eagerly at the oast, though Brenda Steadman remembers Fred Excell dolling out money from his front window when he was living at Abbey Gate Cottages.

Setting up the framework of the hop garden in the first place was quite an art. Many tall upright poles linked together by wire, and then literally miles of hop string for the hop bines to grow up. If it was not all set up properly then a high wind or the weight of the fully grown hop bines could cause a costly collapse. That is where the skills of ladies like Betty Kirby up on her stilts and fastening the strings was so important. Pat Sandford remembers her teaching him how to train hops, which wind round in the opposite way to runner beans. When all the hops had been picked those miles of spent string were gathered up by Peter Kirby and pals and tied together until it stretched from Tyland Lane up towards the Downs and then back again. Then they wound it all up into a huge ball of string that was too heavy to lift. One interesting point is that to firmly anchor the end poles of each row a heavy log was buried in the ground and secured to them. Each log was called a deadman, and in Tyland Lane would be buried close to Deadman's Shaw. Is that another theory for the name given to the woodland!?

In time hand picking gave way to machines doing the job. The bines were now brought by tractor to a shed close by the oast and a machine got to work. As Peter Kirby recalls "Many local woman helped on the sorting conveyor but nothing compared to the atmosphere of the hand picking days, when dozens of people would arrive in the back of the old Army lorry to be disgorged into the gardens for a day's picking".

But then growing hops at all became uneconomical. In 1967/68 the Beebys felt forced to give up growing them, and Haydn Beeby remembers how sad his father Bob was to be dismantling everything and ploughing the gardens up. When Edward Eckley arrived to take over Boarley Farm in 1968 he found all the hop gardens gone, but the oast was to see action for one last time. Maidstone had suffered severe flooding and Cliffords by the river (who were still making hop pockets and many other agricultural items) had carpeting and many goods damaged. The oast's fires were lit and Cliffords' sodden bits and pieces dried out.

By the 1960s, no more picking in the hop gardens. Inside a shed the bines are stripped by a machine. Here Fred Excell at work.

Then the ladies would pick over the hops to remove leaves.   *(Both pictures Eileen Hook)*

The Oasts circa 1950 above.   *(Eileen Hook)*
And below in 2012. Converted to residences.

How better and who better to say farewell to these Sandling hopping days than to finish with a poem written by Betty Kirby.

When all is quiet, I like to remember,
Those friendly hop-fields in early September.
The aroma of hop bines, so rare and so heady,
The Measurer calling, "Get you hops ready".

With all help gone home, the bines all pulled down,
We are left to the country, they've gone back to the town.
Sparrows are searching for crumbs left behind,
By children and pickers, so much to be found.

Soon, when the frosts come, the bins put away.
Ploughing the ground is the task of the day.
Bines neatly cut, the winter to rest,
Their yield for the year so fruitful, their best.

Time now for mending the bin cloths and sacks,
Work for a wet day, with needles and tacks.
Hops pressed in pockets stacked neatly in rows,
Now time to sharpen our knives and our hoes.

Another year past, so quickly they go,
The memories so clear, it does not seem long ago.
Yet time has gone by since those days in September,
But now and again, I remember, remember

Betty Kirby.   *(Peter Kirby)*

An aeriel view of Boarley Farm believed 1950s. Boarley Cottage bottom left next to the cobnut platt. The farmhouse centre. Note the large number of farm buildings to the right. (Ken Marshall and others)

CHAPTER 13

Boarley Farm

Boarley farmhouse sits idyllically at the top end of Boarley Lane and nestling at the foot of that part of the Downs known as Boarley Warren. Daevid Hook's research found it described in 1805 as "a very old farmhouse, two barns, a stable and cart lodge, all thatched". Not long afterwards it was described as "gone entirely to decay". The landlord then was Lord Aylesford, with whom a new tenant arranged that in return for paying a higher rent Lord Aylesford would extend and repair the farmhouse. What we see today is a completely re-built brick exterior hiding some internal parts going back to the 1500s.

Quite sometime after the present tenant farmer Edward Eckley moved in he was intrigued to notice that on the summer solstice the morning sun shone through the front door fanlight and lit up a spot on the floor. A back door was down the opposite end of the hall, and at the winter solstice the setting sun did a similar thing there. Pure chance, or did someone align the building to achieve this?

Across from the farmhouse is Boarley Cottage which dates to the early 1600s. Now one dwelling it was for the majority of its long life split into two agricultural dwellings.

By 1900, Boarley Farm was in the ownership of the Style family as part of their Boxley House Estate. Two brothers by the name of Brooker became the tenant farmers, and Olive Viggers remembered frequently walking from her home in Upper Fant Maidstone all the way to visit her uncle George Brooker at Boarley farmhouse. She also remembered picnics up on Boarley Warren and gypsies coming to help at harvest time, when they would camp in tents and have their fires going at night. The Yew Tree pub would lay on teas for the harvesters. The other Brooker brother lived at the farmhouse on Tyland Corner which later became divided into the three Tyland Cottages.

Around 1936 the Beeby family arrived, dad taking the tenancy and the young sons Dennis and Bob arriving to run the farm. Bob described the farm buildings as being in quite a state, over-run with rats which over the course of several weeks he shot at the rate of some forty a day. Up on the Downs the ground was thick with rabbits, who so nibbled the grass that Bob saw it as resembling courts at Wimbledon. The Beeby family ate a lot of rabbits!

It was a true mixed farm then, growing hops and corn; having orchards of plums, apples, pears and greengages; currants, and a cobnut platt. There were cattle, pigs and sheep, and chicken and geese. Up until the 1940s the heavy work was done by horses, and Stuart Murray remembered six shires, all kept in the stables which still stand opposite Boarley Cottage. Until he died in 1939, the shires were shoed by Harry Mills

Boarley Farmhouse in 1945.

at Boxley village, which was not too far to go. Afterwards a blacksmith was used at Lidsing right over Boxley hill, and Stuart Murray recalls leading two of the shires across the fields to Boxley and up the hill.

During the Second War a Land Girl named Doreen who had come from the East End of London was told to take a shire to Lidsing for shoeing. Instead of using Boxley hill she created her own shortcut by going directly over Boarley Warren. Maybe it was this impressive achievement which led Bob Beeby to marry Doreen. When Pat Sandford came to work at Boarley Farm in 1944 people were still talking about Doreen's shortcut, and the wagoner Jim Checksfield was cross that she had been given the task. Pat can still remember the names of three of the shires. There was Darky who was very wide, Diamond who was a mare, and Timoshenko who was for some reason named after a Russian Marshal.

Lidsing by now perhaps being considered too difficult to get to, Pat aged sixteen was told to take Darky to a farrier at Aylesford. Off Pat set, leading Darky along Tyland Lane, up Veitch's Lane and down into Aylesford where a very wheezy farrier did the shoeing. On the way back Pat decided to spare his feet and ride Darky. Although there was no saddle he could hang onto the halter, though he was sat very bow-legged on Darky's great girth. Pat chose a route home along Forstal Road, and passing Cobtree co-

Two shires being led past Boarley Cottage, early 1900s. An old thatched barn behind.
(Heather Rooke)

The approach to Boarley Farm in 2012.

incided with feeding time for the lions, who began to roar. At this noise Darky suddenly bolted, throwing Pat off and disappearing down the road. Pat trudged back to Boarley Farm, fearful of the trouble he would be in for losing a shire. But when he eventually drew level with the stables, there was Darky in his stall. Pat's greeting from the farmhands was – "Where have you been? Darky got back half an hour ago".

After living for a short while at Tollgate Cottage (which was then part of the farm) Bob and Doreen Beeby settled down to married life at Boarley Cottage, bringing up their two sons. Doreen was not to be kept away from the horses, up at 4.30 in the morning to see to them. In later years Haydn Beeby remembers his mum milking the one cow which was kept near the farmhouse for family needs, and making butter. And needless to say Doreen was also in charge of the chicken. The cobnut trees were close by Boarley Cottage and Haydn became familiar with the constant grunting of the pigs who were kept there.

Bob and Dennis's father had been manager at a training farm at Goudhurst where disadvantaged boys could learn farming skills. This was run by Fegan Homes, and was in the same location where Blantyre House Prison was later to be. Several Fegan boys came to work at Boarley Farm, including Wally Bishop for a short while and Aubrey Tandy for many years. He was a general stockman, known to Peter Kirby as Nunkie, and someone who never seemed to take any time off. After his parents died, Dennis Beeby lived in the farmhouse with his pigeon loft nearby, although the pigeons seemed to prefer sitting on the power lines in the lane.

Peter Kirby spent many hours both playing and helping out on the farm. There was an unusually large number of barns and outbuildings which made wonderful play areas

Bob Beeby at work above.
And below, harvesting close by Boarley Cottage. (*The Beeby family*)

for Peter and the Beeby boys. All around was a varied and lovely countryside. Space to camp; enjoy birds and wild flowers, trees and bushes, help yourself to the over – abundance of fruit; learn to shoot and fish; and ride motor-bikes in teen-age years. Fruit pickers would arrive, and others to pick cobnuts. Brenda Steadman's mum used to be nervous of all the pigs in the cobnut platt, snaffling what had fallen. One lady used to arrive with a bottle of gin and sometimes end up asleep in the hedge.

Boarley Farm has many intriguing field names, which are in danger of being forgotten as hedges are removed and memories fade, though Ordnance Survey still show some. Stony May is in the farm's north-west corner. Where the cricket ground once was is unsurprisingly called Cricket Field. North-east of the Abbey is Bushy Field, where a small hop garden used to be. To the west of Bushy is Cow Meadow, and Haydn Beeby tells that after the war a glider landed there and was immediately surrounded by inquisitive cows who began licking at its many patches of grease. The captive pilot had to be rescued by Bob Beeby.

Eileen Muffett tells of Windmill Field which is a reminder of the Boxley windmill which used to stand somewhere near the footpath which runs westwards of Boxley village. That footpath is on the line of a supposed Roman trackway which is said to have begun from the foot of Bluebell Hill and run eastwards past Boarley farmhouse and on past Boxley church and beyond.

In part of Boarley Warren and by Pilgrims Way there used to be a cultivated area of land used by Shell Research as a "Test Field". Apparently experimental crops were grown, and John Allison remembers a warning notice – "Do not eat produce from this field". What an odd location.

Guests of the Beebys for a while were the Royal Engineers from Medway towns who came to do some fox hunting. The zoo animals across the Chatham Road had an insatiable appetite for hay and the farm helped to keep them supplied.

Edward Eckley arrived to take over the farm in 1968, by which time the farming world had changed dramatically. Mixed farms were now becoming a thing of the past. Whilst still in the hands of the Beebys many aspects were uneconomic, with some of the orchards being picked less and less. The concept of Pick Your Own had not yet arrived. In Peter Kirby's opinion, much of what the Beebys did was for the love of it, as much as to make money. Now Boarley Farm is all arable, and with a long slash of its land taken away by the High Speed Railway.

Edward Eckley outside Boarley Farmhouse in 1998.

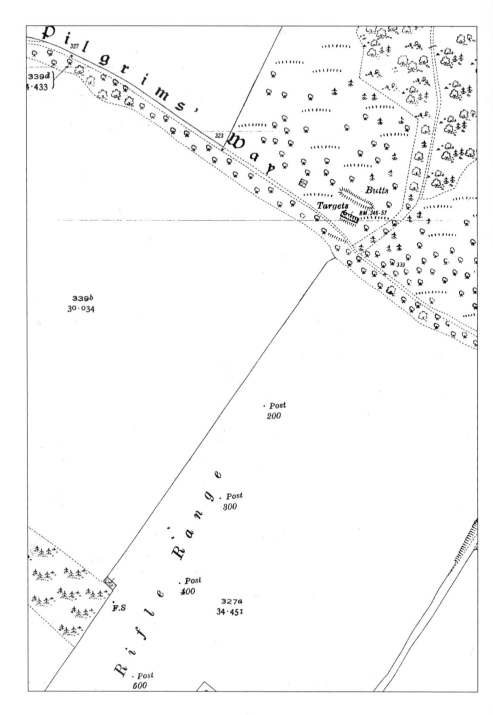

CHAPTER 14

Shooting and Spring Water

Boarley Farm was host to two contrasting forms of shooting. To the west of the farmhouse there was for many years from the 1880s an Army firing range which was rented by the War Office. Maps show various distance posts leading to targets and butts just below the Pilgrims Way. The butts can still be found, and up until the late 1930s local boys used to harvest the lead shot. Ted Kirby's sons would use the lead as weights for their fishing lines, but this game was ended when the Boxley Pumping Station was built in 1938 and tons of the excavated chalk was dumped along the Pilgrims Way. Some of the lead once found was said to have come from blunderbusses. Peter Kirby understands that further west was once a separate pistol firing range.

The range was not used continuously (though Stanley Shrubsole remembered going there around 1930 with a brother who was in the Territorial Army) but came very much to life during the Second War. In the adjacent fields farming would be in full swing. Betty Kirby and other Land Girls would be lifting potatoes and find raw recruits losing control of bren guns and spraying bullets all over the place. Bob Beeby was chatting to an officer one day whilst firing was in progress when the officer suddenly screamed "Stop firing!" He had spotted a nurse riding a bike along the Pilgrims Way. Another version of the tale, or even another occasion, has a nanny pushing a pram towards the line of fire. Edward Eckley was told of one such drama by Sir Leslie Doubleday. There used to be a little hut by the rifle range where ammunition was stored. Edward will tell you that cartridge cases are still being ploughed up.

From the early 1900s until his death in 1945, Bob Style from Boxley House was the landowner. Boarley Farm was but part of his Boxley House estate which stretched from the Chatham Road across towards Detling. Nigella Kent was told on very good authority that he planted a pine tree in each of the four corners of his estate.

Tommy Thompson remembered Bob Style as a big built man who would move between the many farms on his estate in the worst of weather with a scarf wrapped round his neck but no overcoat. The Boxley House estate was famous for its partridge and pheasant shoots, reckoned in their time to be amongst the best in the county. Prominent figures such as Lord Cornwallis and Lord Bearsted would bring their guns. Colonel Winch from the brewery would arrive in a red Rolls Royce. It is Bob Style who is understood to have planted as cover the strip of woodland at Boarley Farm known as The Belting which runs from the site of the rifle range west towards the foot of Bluebell Hill.

When the estate was up for sale following Bob Style's death the auction particulars made much of the shooting and quoted that in the last pre-war season of 1938/39 347 partridges, 496 pheasants, 289 pigeons, 416 rabbits, 30 hares and some 50 "various" were bagged. Shoots took place all over the large estate, but Boarley had its fair share.

The beaters were usually workers on the estate, such as Tommy Thompson who arrived in the late 1930s. He recalled an occasion when Bob Style's gun barrel became so hot from continuous firing that he took his cap off and held it in the cup of his hand as protection. He was apt to fly into a temper if the beaters did not keep in line. Mrs Style would often appear in a pony and trap to collect the fallen game. Amos Golding recalled shooting parties every Wednesday and Saturday from November to March. The beaters would snack on cheese and corn beef sandwiches and celery washed down by Style and Winch beer. Over Christmas they were treated to tots of gin. If the beaters found an egg in a nest they were paid one shilling for it, and the egg was given to a broody hen for hatching and rearing.

Ted Kirby sometimes joined the shoots, and was a legendary shot. Peter Kirby tells the story of his own father Gordon taking a young Peter and an ageing granddad Ted out for a shoot. Ted being too old to walk very far, they left him to rest under a tree with a few cartridges. Having moved on they heard shots in the distance and upon returning found dead pigeons laying out in the field. He had made every shot count. Alan Veitch rated Bob Style a very good shot, able to pick off snipe who flew with twists and turns. Bob's daughters Betty and Ursula were also good shots and often joined the shoots.

The springwater at Boarley has always had exceptional purity. The 1897 map shows watercress beds, and then more significantly the reservoir of Maidstone Water Works. The company acquired four Boarley chalk springs in 1885, which were collected in a covered reservoir which sat within an enclosed compound. The water was chlorinated and fell by gravity all the way down to Maidstone. There was a smaller compound to the east set within what became known as Waterworks Wood, and having a covered well. At one time the company employed Fred Sage to look after these areas. Now this Fred Sage must not be confused with another Fred Sage who lived in Boxley village and helped look after Abbey Farm and Street Farm. Our Fred Sage lived at Ringlestone and cycled to Boarley and had as his base within the main compound a small brick building complete with fireplace and other comforts. The compound contained a large variety of apple trees, and

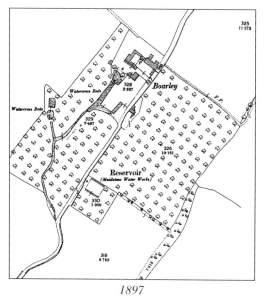

1897

81

Fred tended these as well as looking after the machinery. There was a little apple store complete with racks, and favoured people as well as Fred enjoyed the crop. In bad weather Fred might invite bedraggled fruit pickers from the farm to take shelter with him. There is a memory of Fred at one period cycling first to check over a facility at Detling before moving on to Boarley. To safeguard the quality of the water the Boarley farmers had restrictions on the use of certain fertilizers.

Fred was always good for a chat, and Pat Sandford remembers him and various farm workers gathering together for a natter and rolling their own cigarettes for a smoke. Some very rough tobacco was used, and they tempted Pat to have a puff, which reduced youthful Pat to coughing and spluttering, and the men to unkind laughter.

Next to various ghostly happenings. One dark night Bob Beeby and others clearly saw from the farmhouse an old lady walking up the lane and holding a lantern. Bob went to investigate, whereupon the lady and her lantern simply disappeared. Ted Kirby told of being up on Pilgrims Way and seeing a lady in grey carrying a lamp, again only to disappear. Up on Pilgrims Way during the war Ted saw a number of strange lights. As it was during the blackout he sought to catch the offenders, but there was nobody there. The lights just disappeared. This was near the Lower Bell, and Bob told of another incident there during the war. A soldier, presumably on some kind of patrol, was so frightened by a collection of lights around him that he dropped his rifle and ran.

There have been reported sightings in the area of "big cats". When the High Speed Railway people were fencing some of Boarley Farm's land off, Edward Eckley saw a large cat-like creature leap over a fence and race away. To him that was not a ghost.

Time to leave Boarley Farm, but in proceeding down Boarley Lane towards the Abbey some brief memories of the house Curlews on the left. Court Lodge Farm at Boxley had been run by Harry Foster, and when he died in 1936 his son Dick Foster took over the farm and the farmhouse. He had Curlews built for his mother to live in, and she is remembered

for her perfect hair and general similarity to Queen Mary. Mrs Foster was joined at Curlews by two unmarried daughters, Evelyn and Biddy. Evelyn when young seems to have been a very fit lady, playing cricket and hockey. Biddy was very active in leading Boxley Brownies and Guides, and would have them for picnics and games at Curlews. During the War either Evelyn or Biddy did some nursing and also made sure that the local Land Girls were not too homesick and were coping alright.

Fred Sage's attendant's building within the reservoir area. *(John Allison)*

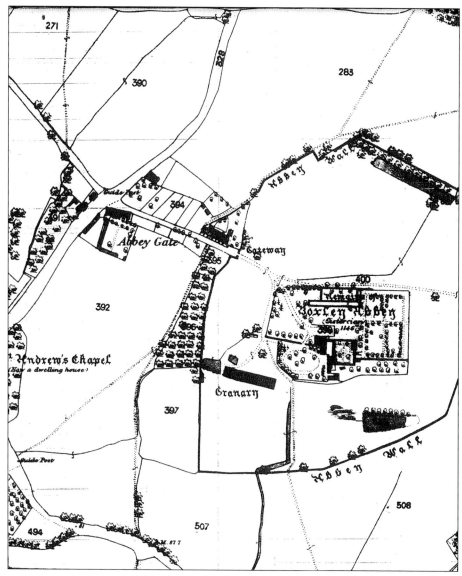

1866. The barn is here called a granary.

CHAPTER 15

Boxley Abbey

After the Dissolution, ownership of the Abbey itself and much of the monastic lands around Boxley were acquired by the Wyatts and then passed in time to the Lords Romney. In the late 1800s Lord Romney began disposing of much of his land, including a sale by auction in 1890 of the Boxley Abbey Estate. This included Abbey Farm, Boarley Farm, Abbey Court Farm, Boxley Corn Mill, the Abbey house itself and more besides. Who bought what does not matter for present purposes, save that the Abbey house was bought by Major Best who was by then happily settled in Park House which he had built for himself in Boxley village.

The Lords Romney, themselves being happily settled in Mote House, had rented out the Abbey house over the years, and Major Best continued this custom by letting to various people, usually of some substance. Major Best died in 1906 and left everything to his niece Lily Best-Dalison, and she too let out the Abbey house. From the 1930s the tenant was Leslie Caldecott, a fellow director with Bob Style in the Style & Winch brewery. He and his wife had three daughters, Kitty, Nancy and Violet.

Elsie Muffett and her family before her have lived for many years in various of the Abbey cottages. She remembers the Caldecotts as a lovely family. They had a very full staff including a cook Moraig who had come down from Scotland, and the kitchen maid Davina who she brought with her; a parlour maid Kitty; various chambermaids and a chauffeur Frank Unwin. As Mr Caldecott drove himself, Frank was mainly there to drive Mrs Caldecott around, though she sometimes used a pony and trap.

When not acting as chauffeur, Frank Unwin helped out in the extensive gardens. But the main gardener was Elsie Muffett's father Fred Owen, whose own father Thomas Owen had been gardener at the Abbey from 1893 until he died in 1946. Fred was wounded in the First War and also served in Ireland, where he met his wife to be. Fred brought her home to Sandling, and when they married in 1927 the two ladies who were at the time tenants of the Abbey house allowed the wedding party to use the grounds, and they themselves disappeared for the day.

From the 1920s until Tom died in 1946 father and son worked together. There is a cottage very close to the Abbey house itself and there Tom and his wife Ellen lived. When her husband died Ellen apparently gave up all interest in life, saying that she would stay in bed for the rest of her days. And so she did, with son Fred or his wife loyally taking in her dinner every day.

Returning to the Caldecotts, they would holiday in Scotland and take some of the maids with them. They all joined in the life and affairs of the wider parish, with Violet

Two views of the Abbey gardens, late 1800s. Tom Owen below.   *(Elsie Muffett)*

The Abbey House with tennis court.

Fred Owen's wedding party in the Abbey grounds in 1927.   *(Elsie Muffett)*

for example being a Guide captain. There used to be a tennis court close by the house, and children from the cottages would be willing recruits as ball boys and girls.

When Lily Best-Dalison died in 1951 the Caldecotts had also died and other tenants had arrived. She left the Abbey to her cousin Sir John Shaw who became Sir John Best-Shaw, and he chose to make the Abbey his new home. Typical of Lily's generosity, certain cottages on the estate were occupied by widows, and she provided that they should be allowed to continue in occupation. As an example, the Bray family had been required by the council to vacate their home at Harbourland and were moved to the other side of Maidstone. Mr Bray had died, and then son John was killed on D-Day. Mrs Bray yearned to be back amongst her old friends in Boxley Parish, and number 3 Abbey Cottages having became vacant, Lily made this available to her, and guaranteed security of tenure by her will.

When the Best-Shaws moved in they also inherited the gardener Fred Owen, who immediately complained that the last occupiers owed him six weeks wages. Sir John got off on the right foot by clearing these arrears, for which Fred was ever grateful. Sir John had been a naval officer, retiring with the rank of Commander. He was an engineer, which as Boxley churchwarden came in useful when the central-heating system at the Vicarage needed sorting out. To help keep him awake during the midnight watch on board ship he took to smoking a pipe. Now ashore at Boxley Abbey, he and Fred Owen began growing tobacco and yielded some good crops. Is it really true that some Best-Shaw grandchildren helped themselves for a quiet smoke?

The younger Sir John remembers how Fred kept all his tools spotlessly clean. And how he literally went out of his way to avoid intruding on the family, never walking up the main drive but crossing a field and making a back approach. Lady Best-Shaw was very puzzled one day when Fred said that he must be off as he had to raise the vicar's salary. By what authority she wondered? Then clues in the conversation revealed that he was going to lift and transport celery from the vicar's garden. As mentioned in an

The wedding of Sir John and Lady Shaw in Malta.   *(The Best-Shaw family)*

Fred Owen.
(Elsie Muffett)

earlier chapter, Fred gave years of devoted service as verger at Sandling Mission.

Sir John and Lady Best-Shaw had seven children, but all of them were grown up by the time the Abbey was inherited. When young the children had a nanny Emily Jane Porter, who "stayed on" and came to the Abbey and took on the mantle of cook. One day she told Sir John that she was doing a treacle pudding which she called hump pudding. Sir John was looking forward to this, and when the time came for dessert he gallantly went to the kitchen to see if he could lift it out of the oven for her. Emily Jane exclaimed "Oh dear! I only made it in my mind!"

Nanny always called Lady Best-Shaw "her ladyship". The story is told that when the motorway was being built, rather too near the Abbey for comfort, that Lady Best-Shaw would creep out at night and move the marker pegs as far away as she could. But those members of the family approached about this disclaim any knowledge.

What everybody knows today as the Abbey barn dates back to monastic times and was originally built as accommodation for pilgrims. Following the Dissolution it fell to agricultural uses, and at one time part was used as a brewery.

The auction particulars for when the estate was sold in 1890 states as follows: "In the Abbey wall on the north side of the garden are two entrances to underground passages which are said to lead to Boxley Church on the east and to Allington castle on the south-west". Surely any passages would never run that far? John Bradford tells of once seeing the entry to a tunnel in the garden wall and being told that it led to St. Andrew's Chapel. Eileen Hook heard tell of the tunnel running in the reverse direction. Brian Tillman and friends once ventured a little way into the tunnel, but turned back when the dark made it too scary. Let us just say that it is one more local mystery.

The Abbey Barn.

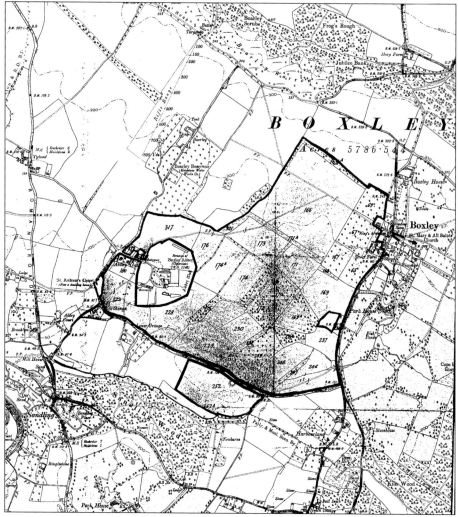

The thick outline shows the lands of Abbey Farm and Street Farm Boxley bought in 1920 by James Clifford from Lily Best-Dalison.

(*James Best-Shaw*)

CHAPTER 16

Abbey Farm and St Andrew's

On the corner of the approach road to the Abbey stands the handsome old building which used to be the farmhouse to Abbey Farm, sometimes also called Abbey Gate Farm or Boxley Abbey Farm. Part of the building dates back to the 1400s. From before the First War this was up until the 1940s home to Jimmy Clifford who farmed both Abbey Farm and Street Farm in Boxley village. His son Herbert was killed in the First War and Fred Owen told of Mr Clifford wandering up and down the road and being absolutely devastated by the news. Mr Clifford was a churchwarden for many years.

In 1941 Wally Bishop was working for Jimmy Clifford, who was by then quite elderly and calling everybody Tom. Wally helped to milk a herd of about thirty shorthorns in the Abbey barn, which had been converted into a cowshed. In the main part were four cow-standings with wooden yokes, and at the other end were two standings with chairs for those milking. There was gas lighting, and the gas was also used to run an engine which crushed barley. It seems that Mr Clifford added a lean-to outside the barn for use as a dairy. His daughter was married to Dr Bernard at Detling, and Wally Bishop was quite often required to cycle all the way there, crossing Penenden Heath, and delivering milk to them.

Abbey Farm farmhouse.

90

Both farms were mixed, and another worker was Tom Shorter. One day in 1941 Tom and Wally were cutting thistles down in a meadow between the barn and Grange Lane. Wally kept coming across pegs driven into the ground and asked what they were for. Tom explained: "They were going to put a road through here but the war came and stopped it". Is it not interesting to know that the Maidstone by-pass was planned in the 1930s? Mrs Mary Collins remembers around the same time seeing similar pegs in the ground at Harbourland, on much the same route as the M20 was to take all those years later.

Another worker was Bill Foreman. Jimmy Clifford had a red Rolls Royce and used Bill to chauffeur him around, such as trips to the bank. A later chauffeur was Jack Beer, and to accompany the grandeur of the Rolls Royce Jack was required to wear mauve livery and leather leggings. Jack used to run Mr Clifford round to Street Farm, and Mr Clifford was puzzled why Jack sounded his horn in Boxley Street when there was no apparent need. Jack didn't like to explain that this was a pre-arranged signal to warn the Boxley men that the boss was approaching. During the war Jack was dressed in another uniform as a special constable. He looked after the farmhouse garden and turned out for the Boxley cricket team. In a short while we shall be meeting his wife.

Jimmy Clifford died in 1946 at the age of 94 (to the last waving his stick at children whose noise was upsetting him) and Abbey Farm and Street Farm were taken over by Mr James Hamilton. As a recent school-leaver, Colin Vaughan went to work for Mr Hamilton in 1951 and confirms the memories of other people that he was a very dapper man wearing a tie and long sleeves with cufflinks even around the farms. Jack Rumble also worked for him and remembers a tall and erect man moving around with big strides and issuing his orders.

It seems that Mr Hamilton was something of an innovator, introducing an unusual breed of sheep and white pigs. Whereas most local farmers had Sussex cattle, he had Aberdeen Angus. Mick Rogers was another worker there and remembers the bull being kept in a bull pen with iron bars. The bull had very short legs, and to serve the cows they had to be stood down in a hole so that the bull could get to his target. Mick would be given the task of training young bulls into obedient ways by walking them round and round the orchard. Another task was cutting the bull's toe nails, which involved a tenon saw.

There were free-range chicken with some thirty or forty chicken houses on wheels in the field. After a few days all the houses were moved, so that in time the chicken droppings had fertilised the whole field. Not so good was that foxes got a lot of the chicken. Mr Hamilton devised a plan of tying an Alsatian dog to a very long piece of string anchored amongst the chicken houses so that it could chase off the foxes. Unfortunately the Alsatian took to killing chicken itself. Maybe for this reason, as Jack Rumble remembers, the chicken were moved inside Abbey barn, which was apparently another innovation. One of Mrs Hamilton's chosen tasks was to clean the very many eggs which were gathered.

The Abbey barn was used as much as in Mr Clifford's time. The family's house cow

Abbey Court Cottages with a hop garden on the corner of Tyland and Boarley Lanes.
(Eileen Hook)

Mr. Hamilton's chicken houses.   *(Eileen Hook)*

92

An old drawing of St Andrew's Cottage. (*Stephen Best-Shaw*)

The same view, probably 1900s. Note the brick letterbox on the left.

93

was kept in there, and it was the place for fattening the pigs. The breeding sows were kept at Street Farm, and Colin Vaughan with the keenness and energy of youth would run across the fields to fulfil his duties between the two. Grain was stored in bags in the barn, many to be chewed open by rats.

It is hard to picture it now, but there used to be a triangle of land set in the road where Tyland Lane meets Boarley Lane, and people remember Mr Hamilton casually parking his motor vehicle there to suit his own convenience. Although some of his innovations caused raised eyebrows, Bob Beeby for one very much respected his farming skills. After Mr Hamilton ceased farming, Abbey Farm's farmhouse was sold for residential use.

On the corner of Boarley Lane and Grange Lane there still stands St. Andrew's Cottage, which in the Abbey's time was St. Andrew's Chapel, catering for the prayer needs of the many pilgrims. After the Dissolution it fell to domestic uses, being for many years divided into two cottages. And then at some date it became a post office.

Over the years Sandling has had a post office in different locations, usually in the Chatham Road area. It may have begun there earlier, but certainly after the Second War St Andrew's Cottage became home to a post office. The postmistress was Jack Beer's wife Florence. She was a local lady whose maiden name was Eaton and who had been in service with Mr. Clifford at one time. Her first husband Albert Baker had been killed in the First War.

The Eaton family at St Andrew's circa 1915. Standing to right are Florence and her first husband Albert Baker who died of war wounds in 1917. Florence was to re-marry to Jack Beer.

(André Plumb)

The Beers lived at St Andrew's and the post office was run from a small annexe with a polished counter. Peter Kirby remembers an elderly Mrs. Beer peering over her spectacles and being very methodical in carefully licking and sticking on stamps. Postal orders needed a rubber stamp which she would carefully prepare and then bring down with an almighty thud. The elder Sir John Best-Shaw remembered her doling out stamps and pensions and "her cheerful bit of local news". She would post letters for people, into the Victorian letterbox set in a brick pillar which she said had been built by her father. Newspapers and sweets were sold.

Mrs. Beer.   *(André Plumb)*

Ann Mutter and other grandchildren remember Mrs. Beer being very strict about their behaviour when they visited, and the post office annexe was strictly out of bounds. To nephews and nieces she was Auntie Floss. There is a tale in the family that when an acquaintance died she was most anxious to make her front parlour available to lay out the body. She was most upset when the deceased was laid out instead in a potting shed.

Apparently a stream ran under St Andrew's to be revealed to visitors by raising a stone slab in one of the floors. In the 1960s there was very bad flooding locally with water lying in the field close by the Abbey barn and elsewhere. It poured into St Andrew's where Mrs. Beer had to raise the precious piano up on blocks. Both Mr. and Mrs. Beer died within ten days of each other in 1969, and that is when the post office is presumed to have closed.

A closer view of St. Andrew's Cottage.

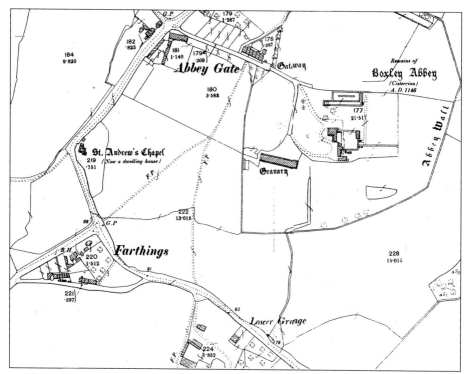

In 1897 The Yew Tree just shows to bottom left as BH for Beer House. Lower Grange Farm's entrance was then off the old pre-motorway line of Grange Lane.

CHAPTER 17

Around The Yew Tree and Farthings

The area around The Yew Tree pub has been known as Farthings for centuries, the name being said to derive from the fairs for selling livestock and produce which the Abbey monks were given permission to hold.

The pub itself probably began its life in the early 1800s as a simple beerhouse. Maureen Waller and her husband became licensees there around 1977 and Maureen points out that the roofing and two staircases indicate that the building was probably once two cottages. There used to be a jug window through which a jug could be filled with beer to consume at home, or children served with ice cream and lollies and sweets. Elsie Muffett remembers a little knocker to gain attention.

Gordon Fullagar's grandfather James Fullagar ran the pub until 1898. He had been a footman at a house in East Peckham, and upon marrying a fellow servant in 1881 was very likely required to leave, as the gentry preferred unmarried servants. The Yew Tree was still quite a simple pub in the 1950s. Tramps would call at the Abbey asking for money, and Sir John Best-Shaw would give them a note addressed to The Yew Tree for them to have a meal. If the offer was taken up Sir John would pay the landlord later.

Gordon Fullagar's family lived for a while in later years at Yew Tree House which is at the start of the run of Farthings and Yew Tree Cottages. He tells of there once being farthing coins fastened on the cottages. Maureen Waller says that until modern fire walls were put into the roof voids of the six Farthing Cottages they were open all the way through. They had been built as farm cottages and Olive Viggers at number 2 spoke of finding straw up in her loft.

Just to the north of the pub, and now having to pass under the intrusive motorway, is the junction with Grange Lane. The coming of the motorway caused the line of Grange Lane to be altered at its western end. Before the re-alignment you would have proceeded east along Grange Lane and come to the entrance to Lower Grange Farm. Now the old farm buildings have become the headquarters for the Kent Scouts, and access from Grange Lane having been denied for years by the motorway, its approach is eastwards of The Yew Tree.

Certainly from 1918, if not earlier, Lower Grange Farm was run by Fred Foster. Upon his death his widow Maude Foster continued to live in the farmhouse but rented out the farmland. She was still known to some as Mrs Fred Foster. The Beebys from

The Yew Tree above, and viewed below from Grange Lane. Both circa 1900.

(André Plumb)

Lower Grange Farm in 2012 as a new home to Kent Scouts. White Cottage, and the roof of the barn just visible.

Boarley Farm ran it for many years, and employed Mr Thompson who lived in White Cottage at Lower Grange Farm. He kept a house cow and would sometimes provide Eileen Hook's family with surplus milk. Pat Sandford remembers him as quite gentlemanly and often wearing a collar and tie about the farm.

In 1968 the farm was bought by Leonard Supple who restored the ancient barn and two long runs of stables, and began to breed racehorses. He died in 2004 and it was in 2011 that the Kent Scouts arrived to bring young life and activity to a very old site. The stables and buildings have been imaginatively converted to a range of uses, including sleeping accommodation, offices and meeting areas.

Back to Grange Lane, and moving eastwards there is just one dwelling, namely Cooke's Cottage about half way along. Maps around 1869 show its location to be a Brick and Tileworks. Bricks once made there are still to be found stamped "Boxley" whilst we are reminded that centuries ago the monks at the Abbey had gained a high reputation for making tiles. Some were used in Canterbury Cathedral, and examples are exhibited at Maidstone Museum. Does the name Tyland derive from tile making?

A large pit was dug out for clay during the brick and tile days, and surprised everybody by filling up with water one night, submerging tools and equipment. Thereafter it became a place for many a person to dump things in or try to fish things out. If P.C. Ted Kirby confiscated a catapult it might be thrown in. After the Second War the Army threw in some ammunition and other items. Jim Ford tried fishing but only hooked up tiles. More successful was Mick Robinson who caught newts, for whom he interestingly used the old word efts.

Cooke's Cottage was originally known as Brick Kiln Cottage, and maybe it was the

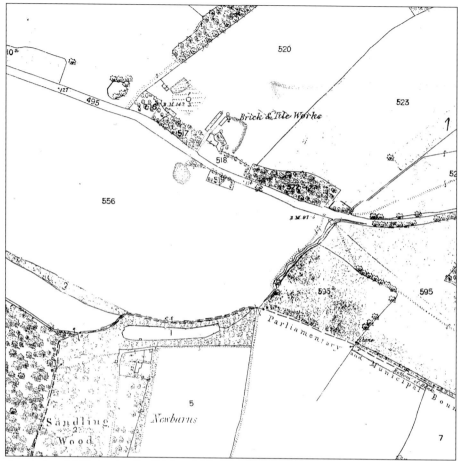

A map circa 1869 showing the Brick and Tile Works in Grange Lane.

works manager's home. Daevid Hook's research attributes the present name to a navy pensioner John Cooke who lived there in 1881, and to some people the road became known as Cooke's Lane, or even Granny Cooke's Lane. And then again, because of the sheepwash further along, as Sheepwash Lane.

Much reference has already been made to Ted Kirby who was the local policeman from 1919 until 1944, and Cooke's Cottage was his home for many years, and where he raised his four sons. As the Boxley book relates, life for the Kirbys there was without today's conveniences. A very deep well had become unusable and so rainwater was collected off the roof, or in dry spells brought by container from Jimmy Clifford at Abbey Farm. An outside toilet of course, lighting by candles or oil lamps, and cooking on a

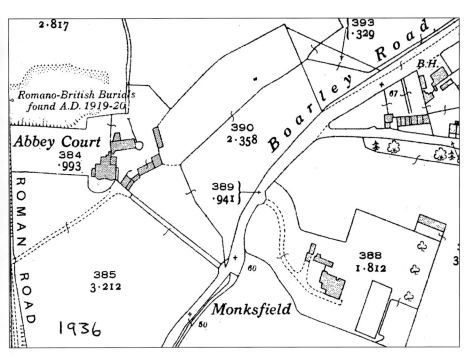

Monksfield.

coal-fired range. One of his sons Bernard spoke of the property having a coach-house and stable, and that the incline in the road nearby became known as Kirby's Hill. Alan Vaughan tells of more rubbish dumping in the vicinity. Right opposite Cooke's Cottage was a tip where once a week rubbish from Park House Boxley was taken by horse and cart and unloaded.

To proceed as far as the sheepwash risks trespassing upon Boxley Village, and so this chapter ends by returning to Boarley Lane and dropping south. We would come on our left to the large house Monksfield which was for many years the home of Mr Farrow and his family. It is thought that Mr Farrow built the house, quite when is not known, but it seems some time after 1909. It had a lot of ground going with it and there is a memory of him having a cowman. By profession Mr Farrow was a chemist based in the Medway towns. Both Eileen Hook and John Bradford remember him creating a series of little waterfalls in the stream running down his side of Boarley Lane and putting in flower plants. Eileen Hook knew this stretch of Boarley Lane as Farrow's Hill. Bill Corner used to cut hay from Monksfield's wide frontage to help feed the zoo animals.

In later years Mr Lidstone came to live at Monksfield, being another businessman from the Medway towns. He and his wife used to hold some lively parties, and there is a memory of guests once dropping in by helicopter. Peter Kirby remembers two bloodhounds which successfully deterred would-be trespassers.

Boarley Lane's stream passes under the little bridge and goes on to join the Boxley stream from Cuckoo Wood on their way to the Medway. Before Dr. Ponder's family created their large pond the little bridge was a place for children to crawl under and splash and play. Eileen Hook was amused one day to see a kingfisher perched upon a board which read "No fishing". Continuing south down Boarley Lane and passing by the Mill house we are once more at The Running Horse.

Sandling, Nr. Maidstone.

A walk early 1900s down Boarley Lane, passing the Water Mill on left of picture.

Stream Cottages above and White Cottages below in 2012.

CHAPTER 18

The Riverside

From The Running Horse we approach the riverside by going along Forstal Road in the direction of Aylesford. The streams that began their journeys from Boarley and Boxley have joined and now pass under Forstal Road. Before doing so the stream many years ago used to power a little mill close by where Stream Cottages now stand. The 1866 map shows it as a mill for sifting seeds, but it had seen other uses long before that. The Boxley book at page 223 sets out its considerable history.

Stream Cottages were built on Garrard's Cobtree Estate and for many years housed his employees or workers on the farms. Fronting Forstal Road are White Cottages which also belonged to the estate. At number 1 there once lived Lady Edna's parents Mr and Mrs Vine. The extensive road works near The Running Horse necessitated the stream passing underground for some distance through a culvert. But whereas in the past rainwater would soak into open ground, it now ran off the large areas of tarmac and concrete and for a time caused the stream to flood into the dip in Forstal Road opposite White Cottages. Mrs Streatfield at number 2 stepped outside on one occasion and stopped the traffic which was causing waves and wash which threatened to flood her home.

Across the road stands large Medway Cottage. Its age is not known but it shows on the 1866 map. Here for some years lived Mr Stewart the vet and his family. We can now make our way down to the riverside itself and the Malta Inn. Until 1950 this was a simple weather-boarded building with a public bar having bare floorboards and a spittoon, and a saloon bar with a carpet, and a small private room or snug. Its customers then were chiefly people using the river or living nearby, including the Ringlestone Estate. In hopping days the pickers across the river would cross at the lock and join the regulars. In 1955 John Percy arrived as landlord and with extensions and improvements put the Malta on its way to what is seen today.

Close by the Malta on the edge of its car park stands the old building which began its life as Sandling Paper Mill in 1714, and later converted to grind corn. It was a water mill and powered by the same stream mentioned at the beginning of this chapter. The wheel went for scrap upon the outbreak of the Second War.

In 1937 Daisy McCabe as a widowed mother moved with her two children Nick and Pat to live in the old mill, re-naming it Malta Cottage. They had been living at Riverside Cottage along the river bank. They had limited resources, and on top of feeding them all Mrs McCabe could barely afford to pay the rent. And so it was that her widower father Walter and her unmarried brother Charles Blackman came to live with them to pool resources. Walter's wife had died in childbirth.

The Malta Inn circa 1950.   *(Daevid Hook)*

RIVER MEDWAY AT ALLINGTON, NEAR MAIDSTONE

Nick McCabe describes Malta Cottage as being divided into two halves. Nearest the river was a living room with a scullery backing onto it, which at first had a window with bars but no glass. On the first floor were two bedrooms and on the second floor a further two. Then there was an attic which became Nick's bedroom.

The other half of Malta Cottage contained the old mill workings with mill stones still there. Both Walter and Charles Blackman were cabinet makers, and Charles was able to make use of the old mill section as his workshop. He specialised in repairing musical instruments and achieved quite a reputation for making batons for conductors. They were tailor-made for individual requirements. When he finally gave up he was asked whether he would pass on his machinery. "Sorry, but I made them with my hands". Charles played the viola and performed with the Old Barn Orchestra at Abbey Court. He died in 1979.

When the McCabes first arrived at Malta Cottage there was no gas or electricity and lighting was by paraffin lamps. But Walter Blackman, well into his seventies, dug a trench all the way to Forstal Road for an electricity supply to be laid. Malta Cottage was sometimes at the mercy of the river when it flooded. Nick remembers the precious piano being raised up on soap boxes, and on one occasion the water was a mere ten inches from the front door. They all sat and prayed, and the water receded.

Just as Pat McCabe described early childhood at Riverside Cottage as idyllic, so Nick remembers Malta Cottage as a happy place. Mum used to take them to the Sandling Mission, seating them either side of her. Nick, as an organist himself in later years, points out that it was not a harmonium that Mrs Kitney played there but rather an American organ. He and Pat would play a game of trying to identify the hymns from the rather unreliable tune that began to emerge. Giggles usually began, and mum would rap their ankles with her walking stick.

Everybody knew everybody in those days, and Daisy McCabe would hear many a tale. One in particular has stuck in Nick's mind. A naughty man had exposed himself to a couple of young brothers, and their concerned mother reported the matter to the police. P.C. Ted Kirby arrived to interview the boys and take statements. Having done so he explained to mum sitting patiently by that he would now read them out before they were signed. He came to the crucial passage that the man "waved his doodlydoo" at the boys. Mum felt a little embarrassed, and then had to hear the same phrase again from son number two's statement. She related all this to Mrs McCabe, adding "if that man comes here again he can wave his doodlydoo as much as he wants, because I don't want P.C. Kirby back".

Another lady called to break the news that her dear mother had died, but stressed it had been a peaceful end. "We sat by mum's bedside, and she suddenly said that she wanted to relieve herself, so we got her up and sat her on the chamber pot. She broke wind, passed a motion, and then expired". What a lovely way to go.

Although people hear of barges moving up and down the river, much trade was carried by small lighters. Several would be linked together and pulled by a tug, but individually steered. They came through the lock on their way to Maidstone and even further. One very common cargo was coal. Nick and Pat were only four and two respectively when their father died. The lightermen knew how hard-up the family was and threw large lumps of coal onto the bank for them. At Christmas the lock keeper would fill a small lighter with logs. It was pulled by men on the towpath and the logs distributed to deserving families. Another occasional gift was a shot rabbit brought by Ted Kirby.

Pat McCabe progressed through Grammar School to University and a teaching career. As deputy head at her old school she was responsible for pastoral care, and she and the head Mary Harvey developed community service out of school hours. Seeing the needs of Maidstone's homeless they took a first step in doing something about it by filling a car boot with soup and sandwiches and seeking out some hungry souls. From this grew Maidstone Christian Care, and for all her charitable and other works Pat came to be awarded the M.B.E. The young girl who collected pieces of coal from the river bank and took her bath in a stream had progressed far.

Further along the tow path is Riverside Cottage. The Boxley book in its chapter about the river gives a full story of this charming building. When the McCabes moved to Malta

Pat McCabe.

Riverside Cottage circa 1900 with mother and daughter Sarah and Rose Wynn who sold refreshments there. *(Daevid Hook)*

109

Cottage in 1937, Riverside Cottage was bought by a relative Jim Rogers. Jim was by trade an ornamental blacksmith, trained and employed by Maidstone's prestigious building firm G.E. Wallis & Son. If one mentions that Jim's handiwork included a spiral staircase at Somerset House and the iron gates to the Memorial Theatre at Stratford then the picture emerges of a master craftsman. Closer to home he constructed the gates to County Hall which lead through to the old Sessions House. His son Mick Rogers says that dad could also do very delicate work, fashioning iron flowers with hammer on anvil.

Jim Rogers, cap askew. (Mick Rogers)

When Jim and his family moved to Riverside Cottage there was no gas, water or electricity. A primus stove was used for cooking and warmth came from log fires. Like the McCabes before them they benefited from lumps of coal thrown from lighters. Every day Jim would go along to The Malta to fetch fresh water, pouring it into a tank. He kept a few pigs which would be slaughtered to help feed the family.

Jim had spent two years as a naval stoker in the First War. He was a considerable character and people remember him always wearing a cap worn sideways, a neckerchief and a leather studded belt. Even indoors he would be wearing his cap. But that belt was never used to punish his sons or daughter. It was quite enough that he took it off and showed it to them. When not in The Malta Jim would sit at the front of the cottage, taking his boots off and standing them beside him.

Jim loved horses and kept several on their bit of land. Sometimes son Mick would have a couple of horses prepared for when dad got back from work. Then father and son would ride up to Tyland Farm, up to Pilgrims Way and along to Boxley. Jim would have a couple of pints in The King's Arms whilst Mick waited outside with the horses. But on Mick's tenth birthday they arrived and as a present dad brought him out a pint of mild and bitter and ten Woodbine cigarettes. The inference was that he was now a man.

When riding between The Running Horse and The Lower Bell, they would use the very wide verge and Mick would sometimes race the Maidstone & District bus, and often win. Mick's ability on a horse attracted the attention of Garrard who for many years led Maidstone's carnival procession on horseback. He enlisted Mick to dress as a cowboy and ride behind him, prancing around and waving a pistol and firing blanks in the air. He was dubbed "the Sandling Kid".

Childhood was open air fun, including a rowing boat on the river, fishing in the Cobtree lake, collecting bamboo canes from Sandling Place's old pleasure grounds in

Cuckoo Wood to be used as arrows. The Maidstone fruiterers Lindridges used to dump out of date fruit in an old sandpit not far from Cobtree's entrance. Mick and other lads got to know the routine and would rummage for bananas and peaches, first chasing away the rats.

From the riverside there still runs steeply up to the main road opposite The Running Horse a footpath. From their home in Ringlestone Crescent the Whale sisters Rosemary, Margaret and Barbara would hurtle down this steep path at risk of not stopping, walk along the towpath and cross the river at the lock. Once over they might wander further to cross the railway line and play in the quarries. And nobody worried. The new lock had been opened in 1937, and the construction work had been a fascination for local children.

At times both old and new locks attracted grimmer attention. The river was a magnet for people intent upon committing suicide, and bodies would drift down towards The Malta. In Ted Kirby's time he would often get a message from his colleagues in Maidstone that a body (which they called "a stiff") was floating down towards the lock and would he fish it out. The bodies were often bloated and swollen and most unpleasant to see. George Brundle would sometimes be involved in wheeling a corpse in a cart to Aylesford where there was a mortuary. A more welcome sight floating down the river was timber from the yard near Maidstone bridge, carried on the then not infrequent flood waters. Jim Rogers made a powerful bow and arrow and "harpooned" pieces of timber which took his fancy and pulled them in.

Jim Rogers gained much admiration over the years by rescuing some nine people in total from the river. Four came at once in the shape of four Americans from Malling Aerodrome being swept along variously inside or clinging to an oil drum. Then there was the unhappy wife who tried to drown herself. That rescue was on a cold and frosty morning, and to help a frozen dad recover Mick was sent to The Malta to fetch a whisky. Her husband was a baker, and Jim did not know whether to laugh or be angry when as a thank you he was given two bags of stale bread for his pigs. In 1951 one of Jim's brave rescues was acknowledged by the presentation of a testimonial from the Royal Humane Society.

Before leaving the riverside, brief memories of the old Gibraltar Inn, now a private residence and lying further along towards Maidstone. During its time as an inn it was patronised by bargees who, before there was an efficient lock, were waiting for the tide to turn in their favour. James Newham, a governor of Maidstone prison, wrote in 1856 of the Gibraltar Inn (known as Gib) being a popular resort for "young Maidstone" and older persons too. Rowing on the river was very popular. Mary Collins heard tales of long ago when the river froze and people would skate between Maidstone and Gib.

Around 1850 a cavalry riding school had been set up at Maidstone barracks, and it was also a depot for cavalry regiments serving in India. The soldiers were used to having two early ports of call on their way to India, namely Gibraltar then Malta. It is said that having walked along the tow path to have a drink at Gib they then made another port of

The old Gibraltar Inn, now Gibraltar House.

call at a hostelry further along and decided that this should be called Malta Inn. Incidentally, we might expect these soldiers to have sometimes included Captain Nolan of Charge of the Light Brigade fame.

The tow path was cared for by the River Catchment Board for whom Bill Laker from Ringlestone worked. He would be in The Malta on Saturday and Sunday nights carousing with Jim Rogers, Mac the bargee and other characters. After closing time you could hear Bill singing loudly and merrily as he made his way home. He would go up a second footpath known as Pepper Alley which starts not far from Gibraltar House. Before the Ringlestone estate was developed in the 1930s Pepper Alley would skirt Ringlestone Farm and take you up to the Chatham Road. Nowadays the footpath travels a shorter distance before linking with Dickens Road.

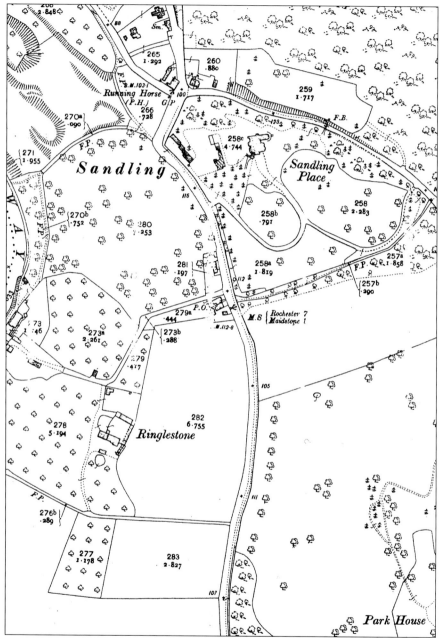

A 1907 map, with the farm Ringlestone having much land, and there being a marked absence of housing.

CHAPTER 19

Down the Chatham Road

If prior to 1930 we were walking down the Chatham Road with The Running Horse behind us, a very different scene would have presented itself compared to today. It is now of course very wide Royal Engineers Road. On the left were Sandling Place's stables, close to the road and which were to remain for many years yet. They occupied the site of the old Red Lion Inn. To our right we would come, as we mercifully still do today, to the ancient timber-framed building "The Old Farmhouse". This dates back to the 1400s.

The Old Farmhouse has seen changes to its use over the centuries, though usually agricultural. In the 1800s it was a farmhouse as part of the Sandling Place estate. In 1859 the farmhouse also became the location for Sandling Post Office in the hands of Henry Fullagar and his wife Charlotte. Their son James became landlord of The Yew Tree in the late 1800s and another son William became butler to the Mercers at Sandling Place. Charlotte as a widow continued to live at the farmhouse and ran a smallholding on the land behind which stretched almost down to the river, and she continued doing so right

Towards Maidstone, with The Running Horse behind us, and the rooves of Sandling Place's stables above the wall. *(Gordon Fullagar)*

Now The Old Farmhouse.

up until her death at the ripe old age of ninety in 1907. The farmhouse continued to be a Fullagar family home until 1945, with William Fullagar tending the land.

In 1945 The Old Farmhouse and its land were put up for sale and the winning offer came from yet another Sandling character. This was William Smith, better known as Trotter Smith, the nickname coming from his collection of high-stepping trotting horses. In 1957 Andrew Rillie's father had built a new house named "Sandyacre" in an old sandpit which adjoined Trotter Smith's land, and Andrew was well placed to observe the activity. A circuit had been laid out, and pulling simple two-wheeled chariots the horses would be put through their paces. This old circuit is now part of the road Castledene.

It seems that Trotter took his horses over to the States and participated in the Kentucky Derby. Back home he took to driving a large American car, but being a small man you could only see the cowboy hat which he wore in place of his usual trilby. He became something of a local celebrity, and for a while The Running Horse changed its inn sign to one showing Trotter and one of his horses.

In the 1960s Trotter organised a trotting track at Detling Showground and large crowds were attracted to see races. But the arrangement did not last for very long. Trotter's trade was dealing in scrap metal, and he always kept his eyes open for new material and opportunities. He was owner for a short while of the old mill up from The Running Horse.

But back to the years before 1930. Just down from The Old Farmhouse and on the corner of Gibraltar Lane there stood a handsome pair of semi-detached houses. The

SANDLING ROAD, MAIDSTONE.

Y & C. 137

Parkes Brothers premises next to the semi-detached houses.   *(Roger and Mary Birchall)*

right-hand one was once the home of Mrs Kitney who played the American organ at the Mission. The house on the left succeeded The Old Farmhouse as being the Post Office for some years and then it became home to the Parkes family, of whom their relative Mary Collins has many memories.

Herbert and Ellen Parkes.
(Mary Collins)

Jack and Herbert Parkes traded together as Parkes Brothers from premises close by the house. Jack was a wheelwright and had separate blacksmith's premises on site, whilst Herbert dealt with bodywork and spraying. Together they built and repaired coaches and carriages, often for the many local big houses. When motor cars became more common they would assemble them for customers, building the chassis, then the bodywork, and finally the inside trim. They built for Beales the funeral directors an early motorised hearse. They also lent their skills in the building of the Mission Church. Mary Collins recalls that the business closed in 1941, and for a while after the war there are memories of something akin to a carpentry business being carried out in the old premises. There used to be a single petrol pump outside,

Parkes Brothers premises on the left.

Parkes Brothers built the bodywork to this Model T ambulance in 1915.   *(Andrew Haynes)*

and now there is a full scale petrol station.

Mary has a few more memories. The house where the Parkes family lived still had at the entrance the words "Post Office" in gold lettering. There used to be wisteria growing up the side wall and one day some monkeys had escaped from the zoo and were clambering all over it. Behind the garage was an outside toilet which had a short door which left wide gaps above and below it. Her grandmother would take her onto Mr Fullagar's land next door to collect cowpats for the benefit of her roses.

The little sign reads "Dann, Boxley, Kent". The cart is selling Ringlestone Farm's milk.
(Jean Allison)

The Ringlestone estate was not built until the 1930s, and up until then Ringlestone Farm complete with cows lay between Gibraltar Lane and Pepper Alley. Most memories are of when the Dann family was running it. The arrival of housing reduced the farm's size in stages and by the 1950s it was really just a smallholding producing fruit and vegetables sold by van. And then it came to be abandoned completely.

Following the outbreak of the Second War both Sandling Place and Park House on the east side of the road were occupied for military and other uses, which we will visit in the next chapters. After the war, when the road was still quite narrow, the activities of the military were very close to the homes opposite. Sandling Place came to be home to the Territorial Army Volunteer Reserve (TAVR). Andrew Rillie's family at Sandymount would be entertained by cadets practising their band music. In Ringlestone Crescent the Whale family were close enough to hear the Army at Invicta Park once a year Beat the

Retreat, with all its noise and ceremony. They were also close enough one day for Mrs Whale's washing to blow off the line and over onto the Army's land. Teenage daughter Margaret was persuaded to cross the road, catch some soldier's eye, and request the return of the articles in question. Margaret has not revealed how intimate some of the items might have been, nor how exactly the conversation went.

The creation of the very wide Royal Engineers Road saw a large strip being taken from what had in the old days been the parklands of Sandling Place and Park House. In the process Sandling Place's stables were demolished. What a contrast it all was to what used to be.

Looking towards Parkes Brothers and showing how narrow Chatham Road used to be.

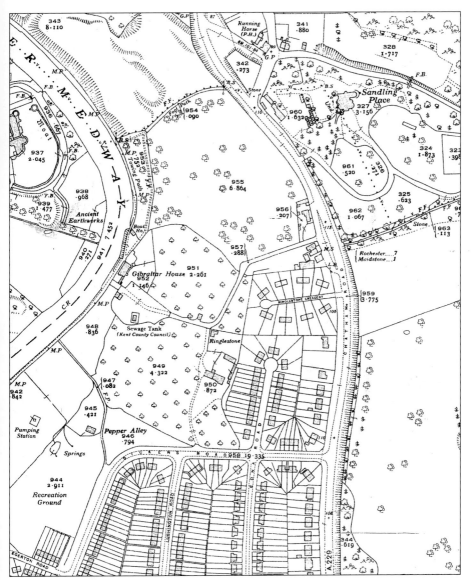

In 1936 Dickens, Lushington and Edna Roads, and Ringlestone Crescent have been built, diminishing Ringlestone Farm and shortening Pepper Alley.

120

The front and one side of Park House in 2004.

CHAPTER 20

Park House Sandling

Sandling's lower part of the A229 in its much widened state is now named Royal Engineers Road in acknowledgement of the military presence in the old parkland. To achieve the considerable road widening, much of the parkland was taken. Until the Second War the whole stretch of the eastern side of the Chatham Road from the junction with Sandling Lane down to a point opposite Monckton's Lane was the land of Sandling Place and of Park House. Both these handsome old buildings still stand, though in completely different settings than of old.

The Boxley book devotes a chapter to the history of Park House under the heading "The Lushingtons", for that family occupied it for over one hundred years. A little more can be added about Edmund Henry Lushington who was the first arrival in 1828. He soon got involved in local affairs, as a magistrate and in helping to establish the West Kent Hospital and the Lunatic Asylum at Barming. He added to the estate by acquiring land on the other side of the Chatham Road stretching down to the river.

Inside Park House.

Edmund was a much loved figure, trotting around his estate on horseback wearing a broad-brimmed hat, inspecting the crops and chatting with his labourers. These included a little bird boy who sat in a simple shelter of hop bines, yelling and shaking a rattle to frighten away the crows. They all knew Edmund as "the Master".

His daughter Ellen recorded these memories, and gives us a glimpse into a rather regimented Victorian life. The family would sometimes have dinner as early as 5 p.m. which left a long evening for them to "enjoy" Edmund reading aloud a Shakespeare play, or a novel or poetry. These jolly evenings would conclude with Edmund saying a family prayer. If a wet Sunday kept them away from Boxley Church then Edmund would conduct a service at home. Indeed, there seems to have been a chapel at Park House, and when the family's departure co-incided with the start of the Second War there is reference to the altar finding its way to Detling airfield.

One of Edmund's sons, his namesake Edmund Law Lushington, married Lord Tennyson's sister Cecilia who in her widowhood led an increasingly eccentric life, as the Boxley book relates. Tennyson was a frequent visitor to Park House and would write in a thatched summerhouse within the parkland. Its position is shown to the left on the 1897 map which appears in the Cuckoo Wood chapter. It was sadly destroyed during the Army's wartime occupation.

Another interior, showing the graceful winding staircase.

The Lushingtons' estate was widespread, down to the river, the allotments close by The Flower Pot pub in Sanding Road, whilst along Sandling Lane they owned part of Cuckoo Wood, land to its west and the old Thornhills Farm which is now covered by Hillary and Bannister Roads. The parkland was known as Lushington Park which the family made available for Sunday school treats and other gatherings. One of the lodge houses still stands opposite the south-east of Cuckoo Wood, and Elsie Parrett remembers as a child living at New Barn Farm on the edge of the wood and knocking up Mrs Nash at the lodge. Then with permission Elsie and her siblings would take a lovely walk down to Park House to pay the rent for their parents. To the west of Peel Street hedges was arable land, orchards, cows and pigs.

By the outbreak of war the Lushington family had dispersed and the Army took over, with an Infantry Training Corps based there. The full title was a Primary Training Centre.

The grand old house became the Officers' Mess whilst the men had a series of huts. What local people had known as Lushington Park was now known to the soldiers as Sandling Park, and in due course as Invicta Lines or Invicta Park.

Whilst at Maidstone Grammar School at this time, Nick McCabe had become Company Sergeant Major in the school cadet force, and a group of the cadets were invited to stay at Sandling Park for a training course and to experience military life. They watched as Regimental Sergeant Major Percy Tasker loudly drilled a large number of new recruits in his very gruff voice. One nervous soldier made a wrong move, and RSM Tasker barked out "Take that man's name sergeant!" Out came the notebook. Drilling continued, and the same soldier once more got things wrong. "Take that man's name again sergeant!" The notebook came out again, and Nick pondered the merits of the same man's name being taken down twice.

The cadets were treated to breakfast in the Sergeants' mess, and could not believe how many eggs and slices of bacon and other trimmings were piled upon their plates. Along came RSM Tasker. "You look hungry. Would you like some more?" And of course they did.

The war having ended, the Army left Sandling Park in 1945 and the site lay vacant for the next three years. Then it became home to the Royal Engineers. As a National Serviceman, Roy Carey was the very first sapper to arrive as part of the advance party.

A gathering of Lushingtons at Park House circa 1930.   (Molly Mitchell)

In one hut they found a store of new issue lightweight green Army blankets which were "liberated", and local girls would be seen around Maidstone and at dances wearing green skirts and coats.

The servicemen spent their spare time in various of the local pubs, mostly The Running Horse which was nearest, and at Star Hotel dances. Things could be a bit rough at The Star on a Saturday night, so much so that you went downstairs to the toilets not alone but rather in a group for safety.

Roy Carey's period of National Service was 1948 to 1950, and he gives 1950 as the date when the Engineers threw the Bailey bridge over the Medway at Aylesford to help relieve the traffic jams there. He just missed the Korean war, but some of a later intake that he knew from Sandling Park were out there clearing mines and were killed by Chinese troops. Whilst the regiment was out of the country the old huts were removed and new facilities built.

Sandling Place was being used by the Territorial Army after the war, and running between the grounds of Sandling Place and Invicta Lines was the footpath known to locals as "cut-throat alley" which linked Chatham Road with Sandling Lane. When the Infantry were around the soldiers returning from a night out would clamber over the fence. After the Engineers arrived there was a hole in the fence which made things easier. Locals now began to call it lovers lane, and the night before his wedding one sapper anticipated his honeymoon night by smuggling his bride-to-be into the barracks.

We now move on for memories of Sandling Place.

An early bus on its way down a concreted Chatham Road.　　　　　　*(Gordon Fullagar)*

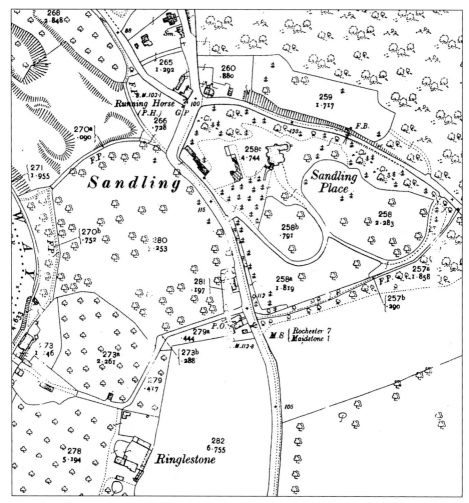

1907. Marked FB is the footbridge over Sandling Lane leading to the pleasure gardens in Cuckoo Wood.
FP markes the footpath known as cut-throat alley.

CHAPTER 21

Sandling Place

From 1859 Sandling Place was the home of the Mercer banking family. It had been built in 1823 and in its early days enjoyed the modest name of Sandling Cottage. Close by and fronting the Chatham Road stood the ancient Red Lion Inn, which Daevid Hook's research for the Boxley book revealed to have its origins going back to the 1500s. It was a coaching inn, but was to lose trade with the arrival of The Running Horse. Daevid thought that it was probably around 1890 that the Mercers demolished the old inn and built stables on its site. More lands were purchased including down to the river and part of Cuckoo Wood. The grander name of Sandling Place was well justified. Gordon Fullagar's mum Edith had been a parlour maid for the Mercers and long after the Second War was talking of "Red Lion field", which shows how memories of lost names and places can persist.

Memories of the Mercer family are from the 1930s. There were two brothers, Randall and Richard (who was often unwell) and Sister Isabelle (who was considered a sweet lady). The Boxley vicar then was Rev. Jimmy Hale, and he and his family used to

Sandling Place after being divided into apartments.   *(Tim Ferris)*

do the rounds on Christmas Day, having luncheon, tea and supper in turn at various big houses. At Sandling Place Miss Isabelle would press coins into the hands of the vicar's children on their many visits, and Morwenna Hale complained to her brothers that they always got more than she did. She was overheard, and matters were corrected on the next occasion. After tea in the summer there would be croquet on the lawn. It was a popular place for them to visit, and when the vicar called on his own he was plied with sherry and departed a little unsteadily.

In a house, later demolished, on the bottom corner of Sandling Lane there lived the Mercers' coachman Mr Brunger, who had very long whiskers. Stuart Murray remembers Mr Brunger transporting the Mercers by carriage even into the late 1930s. Apparently not unusual for the time, and Stuart remembers Louisa Whatman from Vinters pulling up in her carriage in Week Street to shop.

The butler was Henry Card, who developed a strong dislike for Randall whom he found too condescending and grand. Every evening after dinner Randall would retire to the lounge to have his coffee. As Mr Card progressed along a passageway on his way to the lounge he would pause to raise the lid of the coffee pot and spit into it. This continued over a long period of time.

Owning as they did part of Cuckoo Wood, the Mercers created in its south-west corner an area of pleasure grounds which included ornamental trees and shrubs and bamboo and grassed areas. Peacocks would strut around and tennis parties were held. To gain access from Sandling Place a very attractive bridge was constructed to span

The bridge over Sandling (once Sandy) Lane.   *(Mary and Roger Birchall)*

129

The Boys' Bible Class being entertained in the pleasure gardens early 1900s. Randall Mercer believed fifth up on the right. *(Gordon Fullagar)*

Sandling Lane, probably in the 1890s. One of Gordon Fullagar's mum's jobs was to keep the handrail clean. Back in the 1920s Randall had given part of the north-west corner of the wood as a site for the Mission Church.

In 1941 Randall died, and it seems his brother and sister had predeceased him. Towards the end Randall became something of a recluse. Henry Card is understood to have become butler to Garrard at Cobtree, and went to live in Stream Cottages with his wife and daughter. The Second War was now in progress and Sandling Place was to undergo a considerable change. For the information and memories which follow we are indebted to Mrs Win Rolfe.

Because Chatham Dockyard was a prime target for German bombers, the Admiralty dispersed many of the civilian staff. The wages section was re-located to a now unoccupied Sandling Place, and that is where sixteen years old Win found herself as a junior clerk.

It seems that upon arrival the staff found no gas or electricity, with oil lamps having been used by the Mercers to light the rooms. Apparently they did not use any motorised transport and refused to have any bus stop nearby. Win was consigned to work in an attic room with a low ceiling and one small window. The sun never seemed to get in, it was gloomy, and the only warmth came from a small Victorian fireplace. In the centre of the roof was an open rectangular area surrounded by inward-sloping roofing, and in the summer months girls could do some sun-bathing there.

One of the clerks had a grandmother who was a maid at Sandling Place in the late 1800s and she had told of the servants sleeping in the attic rooms with two beds to a room and two persons to a bed. She also told of the attic being bitterly cold in winter and stifling hot in summer. Away from the summer months Win found it "a cold and cheerless house". The small Victorian grates did not take much coal (which was rationed anyway) and no fires could be re-kindled after 2.30pm.

Win described the dining room having large wooden shuttered windows, and the drawing room had gilded framed mirrors hanging above a large fireplace. From the lounge there were French doors leading into a Victorian conservatory, which though dilapidated was still housing a grape vine. Win reckoned the largest room in the house to be the billiard room, whilst her references to the butler's pantry and a gun room give us still more of an impression of grand lives having once been led there.

There was a "double layer" of cellars tucked beneath the house. Here the old servants' hall would have been located, and now it became a staff canteen. Mid-day meals might be mince and veg, or stew, or meat pie. The smell of over-boiled cabbage would permeate the building. Down in the cellars was an internal well, and Win related this story, confirmed also by one of her friends:

"One lunch-time three of the younger men took it into their heads to find out if there really was a secret passage leading from the well to the stables down by the main road. To prove the story, two of them lowered the third by his ankles over the side of the well where he found the entrance to the passage and by torchlight made his way along and up through a trapdoor into the stables, startling the girls working there".

And then there were the ghost stories told to the girls. That the grounds were haunted by a young woman who, rather than marry the husband chosen for her, flung herself from the bridge over Sandling Lane. And the ghost of another young woman on a white horse on her way to elope with her lover. And the old smuggler who hung himself from the bridge rather than be caught by the Excise men. Elsie Parrett, who lived near the eastern end of Cuckoo Wood, also heard tales of the bridge being haunted. Overhanging trees made it very dark, and she and her siblings would only pass under it if accompanied by their mother.

The Admiralty staff returned to Chatham after the war, and Sandling Place fell to quasi-military uses. By 2004 it was vacant and Jeremy Lawson led the re-furbishment of the whole building with a view to creating separate apartments within the old house. Previous occupiers had partitioned off some of the large rooms with blockwork which had to be removed. Lovely old coving to ceilings had to be matched and repaired, whilst long runs of deep pine skirting boards needed hours of restoration. It is a cause for rejoicing when old houses survive, in Sandling Place's case by adapting to modern living requirements.

A wartime picture showing the conservatory.   *(Win Rolfe)*

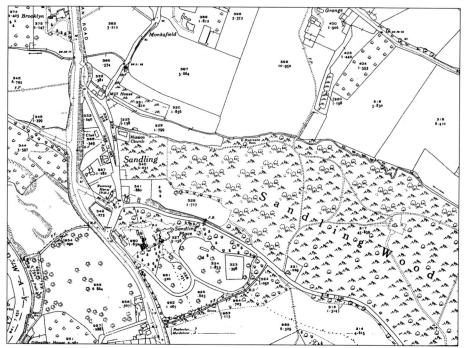

The 1936 map shows Cuckoo Cottage where footpaths converge on the right, and the cottage The Chestnuts where a footpath leads in from Sandling Lane.

CHAPTER 22

Cuckoo Wood

Cuckoo Wood appears on early maps as Sandling Wood. Daevid Hook discovered that in the 1880s a gardener named John Cuckow was living in a cottage in the wood, and one can imagine local people attaching his name to the woodland, and then the name becoming corrupted to Cuckoo Wood. Ordnance Survey knowing none of this would have kept to the original name, but eventually caught up with local custom.

That cottage in the wood became known as Cuckoo Cottage and was last inhabited by Mr & Mrs Minto into the 1960s. Many years earlier it was home to John Brodie who was a gardener at Sandling Place, which is doubtless where John Cuckow was also employed. Chris Hunt is a descendant and heard tell that Mr Brodie was an exceptionally tall man, and that he would walk across the little bridge to get to his work at Sandling Place. He would have tended the Mercers' pleasure gardens in the wood as well. Chris Hunt's parents used to visit Cuckoo Cottage, and told of it being surrounded by bluebells and birdsong. It is long since gone, though it is possible to identify the position by a very small amount of debris. It had a well. Ivy Brodie, daughter of John and Louisa Brodie, is understood to have married Ted Kirby.

John and Louisa Brodie at Cuckoo Cottage. *(Sue Hunt)*

There was another cottage on the southern edge of Cuckoo Wood close to where the "cut-throat alley" footpath joins Sandling Lane. A handbook "Kent's Capital" of 1899 suggests a ramble in which you enter Cuckoo Wood (note the use of the name) by "an old wooden cottage". This came to be called "The Chestnuts", and like Cuckoo Cottage it was constructed of black weather-boarding. Elsie Muffett like others knew it as Black Cottage and she remembers Philip and Winnie Croft living there. When Sandling Lane was widened in the 1950s it was also straightened to some extent, leaving The Chestnuts marooned with the old road on one side and the new one on the other. It is said that Crofty, as he was known, refused to move, but in time the dwelling was demolished. The old stretch of road is now overgrown and lies close against the fence to Invicta Park.

The bridge over the stream in Cuckooo Wood.

The waterfall in Cuckoo Wood from "Kent's Capital" of 1898.

It was with the road-widening that the lovely old bridge was removed. It is possible to find part of its support on the bank on the south side of Sandling Lane. Ownership of Cuckoo Wood was once divided between the Mercers of Sandling Place and the Lushingtons from Park House Sandling, the latter family once doing some shooting in there. Ted Kirby trained a gundog for them.

John Luckhurst and others of the Luckhurst family came to know the wood very well. Close to 1900 there was a football pitch located towards the south-west corner. The stream which rises in Boxley flows through the northern edge of the wood, and an old map calls it the Boxley stream. In the north-east corner near New Barns there used to be a sluice with brickwork and an iron grill which could be raised to control the flow. Around this was a very watery area known locally as "black swamp". The stream seems to have been diverted around the sluice at some time, probably for the following reason.

When the Boxley waterpumping station became operational around 1938 the extraction of water made for a drastic reduction in the flow of all local streams. The handbook "Kent's Capital" mentioned earlier contains an almost unbelievable picture of a waterfall in Cuckoo Wood which could only have been the result of a considerable rush of water. Ted Kirby's son Bernard told of catching trout in this stream before 1938, just as Bob Luckhurst told of doing the same in a stretch of the stream near the sheepwash. Sometimes the fields nearby would flood.

These days it is quite challenging to walk beside the length of the stream, some agility being required. One of the most interesting features is the stone bridge which carries the footpath from Sandling Lane over the stream and on past Lower Grange Farm. Bob Luckhurst told of this being the route that monks or visitors travelling by river would have taken to get to Boxley Abbey. Perhaps disembarking on the bend in the river by Gibraltar House, moving east to cross the old Roman road, up "cut throat alley" and then through the wood to the bridge.

The bridge has a pointed arch which is a feature said to have appeared In England in monastic churches from around 1170. Boxley Abbey was founded in the 1140s. The bridge is wide enough for a wagon to pass over. The theory is advanced that somewhere between the 1100s and 1400s it was built for the benefit of the monks.

Another interesting feature to be found is the remains of the hydraulic ram which is shown on maps just west of the bridge. A dictionary defines this as "a pump that forces running water to a higher level by utilizing the kinetic energy of flow". A valve is also involved in the process. A lot of trouble must have gone into building and maintaining it, but for whose benefit? Was it for Sandling Place? The Boxley stream runs on to the old mill in Boarley Lane.

Sand was once excavated from a very large pit to the west, where are now the houses of Sandbourne Drive. When the Royal Engineers first arrived at Sandling (otherwise Invicta) Park they would run for fitness through Cuckoo Wood. One day the leading sapper stopped in his tracks at the unseemly sight of a soldier and a lady from the NAAFI in a very compromising position in the sandpit. One hopes that the crocodile of sappers

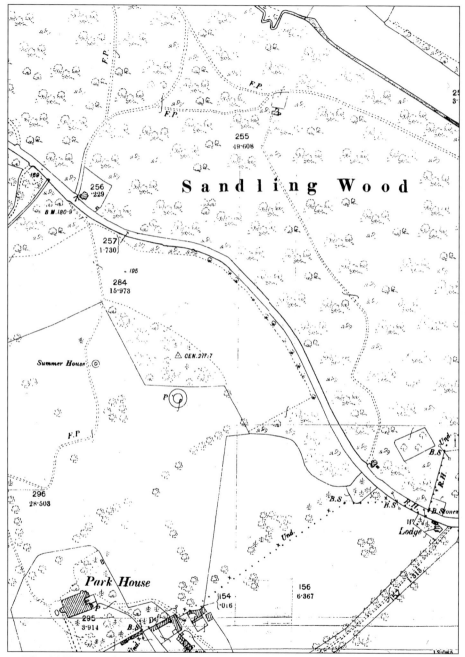

The 1897 map shows at middle left the summerhouse where Tennyson wrote.

behind him passed by with eyes averted. In fact there were cheers and shouts of encouragement.

Most of the trees are chestnut for coppicing. Particularly large areas were cut down in the 1940s and again in he 1960s, when a lovely view was opened up to the Downs, causing motorists to pull up and admire it. Sandling Place's old pleasure gardens in the south-west lay neglected after the Second War, with the various ornamental shrubs struggling for survival. The little bridge survived for a few more years, but its purpose had gone and the entrance was boarded up. Somebody kept pigs close by it for a while, fenced in with barbed wire.

The Mercers and Lushingtons having departed, there was now "free entry" and holly would be gathered at Christmas and large branches for Guy Fawkes night bonfires. It was a good place to gather bean poles and pea boughs, though one man was stopped by the local policeman and told to go and put his armful of pea boughs back where he had found them. In the Spring, and when it was no offence to do so, people would emerge carrying armfuls of bluebells. At one time a cycle track was created, and at another time even motorbike trials took place. The old pleasure gardens were to see residential development arrive, first the tall block of Boarley flats and later Burleigh Drive, Cuckoo Wood Avenue and Sandbourne Drive.

Close to the eastern edge of the wood used to lay Newbarns Farm, which was more of a smallholding. Elsie Parrett was brought up in the 1920s in a thatched cottage on the farm which was reached by walking from Sandling Lane along what they called "rough stones path". She remembers the land being worked by Bill Fullagar from Ringlestone, and he and his dad would clatter down the path in a horse and cart. When in 1923 at the age of four Elsie had scarlet fever the ambulance was unable to drive down and she had to be carried in a blanket to Sandling Lane. The disease being very infectious, she was many weeks in the West Kent Hospital and when mum visited she was only allowed to look at Elsie from behind glass.

The cottage had just two bedrooms, with mum and dad sleeping in one with their only son, and Elsie and her four sisters sleeping in the other, three girls in one bed and two sharing another. Mum had these six children within the space of nine years. She would wash them all in a tin bath, the son getting in last, and then she would comb all their hairs on the lookout for nits. She would walk all the way into Maidstone to shop and walk all the way back again. The sheepwash in Grange Lane was a short distance away and where the children would paddle and splash. Elsie recalls that the family were "so poor and so happy".

Around 1930 Bill Fullagar gave up Newbarns Farm and it was taken over by the Pearce family, and this necessitated Elsie's family having to move out.

Eileen Carey was living in another cottage at Newbarn Farm during the Second War, and she remembers the Pearce family running their smallholding. She and other children were allowed to feed the cows and pigs, whilst there was an old double-decker bus on the land which they would all delight in clambering over. The Pearces built an underground

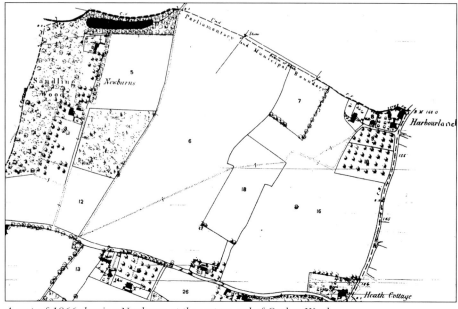

A map of 1866 showing Newbarns at the eastern end of Cuckoo Wood.

The Sheepwash in Grange Lane. 1904. (J. B. Groom)

air-raid shelter with tunnels, and Eileen's memory is of soil constantly trickling upon her when down there.

For some years spanning the war there used to be in the south-east corner of the wood Kath's Café, a simple building with a large forecourt. It took the chance to cash in on custom from the heavy traffic using Sandling Lane before the by-pass was built. But Elsie Parrett remembers that around 1930 Sandling Lane was fairly free from traffic.

During the war one large bomb fell in long meadow on the northern edge of the wood, creating a huge crater which remained unfilled for some years. It is said that a second bomb fell in the wood but never exploded. Which leads us into the next chapter.

Coming down Sandling Lane towards The Running Horse.

Guarding debris from the German bomber which crashed near the Abbey in 1943.

CHAPTER 23

The Blast of War

On the 3rd September 1939 Nick McCabe aged eleven and Pat McCabe aged nine had been picking pears at Sandling Farm when an air-raid siren sounded for the first time. Young as they were, they had both known that war was imminent, and now it was clearly happening. The two worried children hurried home, and very soon the family was building to its own design an air-raid shelter on the edge of the stream by Malta Cottage.

George Brundle at Sandling Farm got involved at an early date. After Dunkirk some boats ferried rescued soldiers up to the lock and set them ashore, whereupon George and his wife billeted them in the oast and fed and clothed them until other arrangements could be made. George would take them to The Malta for a drink, and as some reward the soldiers dug out an air-raid shelter for him. When a siren sounded it was two sheep dogs who got down there first.

Then came the Battle of Britain, and Dinah Reid recalls seeing a German parachutist floating down towards the zoo park. Knowing that he would have a pistol and not knowing where he might land, all the girls were rushed to Cobtree Manor where a very large trapdoor was opened and they were all hustled down into the cellar for safety. The parachutist drifted further away. It may have been this German, or perhaps another on a separate occasion, who landed at Sandling Farm. That airman fell onto the roof of Sandling Farmhouse and broke one or even both legs. Regular soldiers arrived to capture him, and one of them accidentally fired his rifle which terrified the German. Dr Heath was at home in the house and he arranged for the airman to be taken to the West Kent Hospital for treatment.

There was fear of invasion, and some open areas were identified as possible landing grounds for German gliders. Northfield on the Cobtree Estate was one, and it was scattered with obstacles. Dinah Reid recalls an occasion when a German plane flew low over the zoo and began machine-gunning. The cry went up "Lay on the ground"! Elsie Muffett heard tell of hop-pickers in Tyland Lane looking up at an approaching plane, seeing the swastikas, and all rushing into Deadman's Shaw for shelter. She is not sure whether it fired at them, but there was admiration for a lone man who simply carried on picking.

The early days of the war saw the creation of the Home Guard and Sandling men had their own platoon, though tied in with Maidstone. Farm work was a reserved occupation since food production was so vital. Sandling's many farm workers, though exempt from military service, were recruited into the Home Guard and met in a hut behind The Yew Tree. Amos Golding told of a time when there were just six of them, three on duty and three off. Numbers increased, and one task was guarding the Boarley water reservoir.

The men still had to do their farm work, which at harvest time was particularly tiring. Home Guard duty was in the evening and Bob Beeby in the Sandling platoon found himself on the go for eighteen hours at a stretch. Patrolling the district was one task, and around the Peneneden Heath area one evening he fell asleep from fatigue. A major prodded him and said this was a punishable offence. Bob protested that eighteen hours on the go was unreasonable, and the major let matters drop.

Eighteen years old Wally Bishop had to be on patrol between 10 p.m. and 6 a.m. and he and one other would patrol up Boarley Lane from The Yew Tree, and eastwards along Pilgrims Way to meet up with two Home Guard men from Penenden Heath, usually the same two. They would all have a chat before each pair retraced their steps to base. One of the Heath men's parting words were often – "if you see anyone I know whose looking for me, just tell them I've gone". At first opportunity Wally volunteered and joined the Navy.

Les Bathhurst from Smith's bakery responded with others to a report that a German parachutist had landed somewhere near the Downs. They nervously set off to search for him, some armed only with knives tied to the end of sticks. They heard some rustling, and one man who did have a gun fired off a shot, only to find that he had killed a cow. It is worth mentioning here that later in the war some regulars on a night exercise bayoneted several sheep.

On the subject of animals, one of Garrard's fears was that the zoo would be bombed. He reasoned that if a cage was hit then the animals would very likely be killed, but he had a particular worry about bears getting loose. Jim Rogers and a few others were asked to be on hand with their rifles just in case. Some animals were sent up to Scotland as a precaution, but the zoo was encouraged to stay open as a place of entertainment. Dinah Reid recalls that soldiers from Maidstone barracks would manage to rendezvous there with family members who lived not too far away.

Plenty of bombs fell around Sandling. Mick Rogers remembers some seven incendiaries dropping in a bunch close by Riverside Cottage. None exploded, and afterwards he watched as bomb disposal people carried them away along the towpath, cradled in their arms. A young Bob Corner would amuse himself by de-fusing live incendiaries which had fallen harmlessly into sandpits. Nick McCabe remembers a bomb falling not far from Malta Cottage and exploding with an enormous bang which crazed the ceiling plaster in his attic bedroom.

The Beeby family at Boarley Farm were central to an incident which has gone down in local folklore. Adding Tony Webb's meticulous research to people's memories the tale can be told. In 1943 a German bomber JU88 with a crew of four was caught in a searchlight beam and hit by flak over the Medway towns. It jettisoned its bombs, killing five people, and tried to fly home. Having cleared the Downs the crew decided to bale out, and as Tony Webb's detailed account relates – "The stricken aircraft zoomed to earth in a steep dive, and engulfed in a ball of fire it crashed in a field north-east of Boxley Abbey".

As to the crew, early the next morning a game keeper at Thurnham found one of them suspended from his parachute in some tall trees and clearly dead. Another was found on the Detling reservoir, also dead. The pilot and fourth member landed safely in the Boarley Warren area, and Bob Beeby told what happened next.

Bob's parents were living in Boarley farmhouse and Mrs Beeby was there alone. She answered a knock on the door and was confronted by a German airman who addressed her in perfect English. "I am sorry to disturb you. I want to surrender. Take my pistol please", Mrs Beeby invited him in and rang P.C. Ted Kirby. Whilst awaiting Ted's arrival she did the English thing and made the German a cup of tea. Ted duly arrived and, having served in the First War and having no fondness for "the enemy", he upbraided Mrs Beeby for her hospitality. He took the German into custody. Mrs Beeby complained afterwards to her family about how rude P.C. Kirby had been.

Ted's son Bernard, who served as a Marine commando and saw some very hard fighting, told that on his way to the farmhouse his father found the fourth crew member trying to hide in a hedge. Home Guard men stood guard over the smouldering wreckage of the JU88 and Ted warned them not to stand too close. Sure enough something exploded and although they were standing well back they were blown into a hedge.

Hadyn Beeby was told of a German pilot crash-landing with such force that his feet were driven out of his flying boots. This was harvest time, and he was surrounded by farm workers with pitchforks held at the ready. Robin Walton recorded an interesting contribution by George Brundle to the war effort. He kept racing pigeons and made these available to RAF pilots at Detling who would take them on flying missions. The intention was that if the pilots crashed, the marked pigeons would somehow be released and return to George who would then hurry to The Malta and telephone Detling airfield.

There is a bit of a mystery about a cluster of huts at Cobtree sited near to where the golf clubhouse is now. It seems that a radio station was run from there during the war and was rather "hush hush". It was run by Redifusion with whom Garrard had a connection, and after the war Radio Luxembourg was picked up and re-transmitted.

The Boarley firing range was in constant use, and Colin Vaughan remembers soldiers marching up through Boxley village and then making their way towards it along Pilgrims Way. Brengun carriers would scoot around at the range, and machine guns added to the noise. There were sentries posted, signs put up and red flags waved warning local people to keep away. As if that was not noise enough, some Anti-aircraft guns came to be placed nearby with searchlights and Land Girl Betty Kirby spoke of what a racket they made. A German fighter crashed just above Pilgrims Way.

The war progressed, and preparations were in hand for the invasion of Europe. Troops were camped all around, for example in Marsh Wood which is now on the edge of the golf course. Security was paramount, and road blocks were set up in various places. There was one on Bluebell Hill which Dinah Reid had to pass on her way to the zoo. The soldiers manning it soon got to know her and hailed her approach with wolf whistles. They always asked to see her identification card, explaining that they were bored and wanted to chat. They would ask her to post letters for them so that the postmark would give their families some clue as to where they were. On one occasion the soldiers mended a puncture for her.

There was another road block between Brooklyn and The Running Horse which Betty Kirby had to pass. She was always stopped despite her protests that "You know me! I'm Betty!" Betty was a young Land Girl which in theory was voluntary work, but girls were expected to become one or to join female sections of the armed forces. Some were as young as seventeen and might be very far from home. Many were billeted with local people. Going back to the road block, embedded in the bank by the side of the road were 40 gallon oil drums, with bottles of petrol dangling in front, to be set alight had the Germans come. Then burning oil would have spread across the road.

The roadblock just below Brooklyn.

Another young girl Win Rolfe was working as a clerk with the Chatham Dockyard wages staff at Sandling Place. Every ten days the girls took turns to stay overnight for fire-watching duties, when eggs and bacon at Kath's café on the edge of Cuckoo Wood were a bonus. In November 1944 the engine of a flying bomb stopped overhead, which was

145

particularly frightening for those of them working up in the attic. We shall tell shortly where it landed, close enough to rattle the windows, whilst "the inkpots danced on the table". One of the older ladies sang some old Music Hall songs to keep spirits up.

The flying bomb hit a pine tree and fell close by the Chatham Road lodge to Cobtree where Netta Jarman and her very young son Danny were at home. It was an enormous explosion and the roof caved in and that is how Netta became partially deaf. She and Danny were trapped in their bedroom by fallen debris, and first on the scene was fire warden Mr Pilkington. It was dark and Pilkie was startled to see a pair of eyes staring at him, which being near the zoo he feared was a lion. In fact it was Netta's cat, but he beat a hasty retreat, leaving the Army to eventually come and rescue them. Garrard used a large fragment of the flying bomb to "decorate" the elephant house and with a suitable message scrawled on it.

Whilst the windows at Sandling Place rattled from this mighty explosion, others for some distance around were broken. These included at Bakery Cottages and in Tyland Lane, whilst a wall at number 1 Abbey Cottages was split. Fire warden Mr Pilkington had another escapade which he told to Linda Ellis and which she has written about. A bomb had fallen at the zoo.

"Pilkie went to inspect the damage. He arrived on the scene to find a couple of mangled, empty cages and a stunned dog wandering aimlessly near the crater. Pilkie, knowing that his neighbour was a keeper at the zoo, called the dog to follow him down the hill to Chatham Road. "Come on little doggie," he coaxed, "Come on little doggie" across the road and into the woman's front garden. Pilkie knocked while the dog waited quietly behind him. The door opened, a woman's silhouette filled the gap for a moment, then the door slammed shut. "Get that wolf out of my garden" she yelled through the letter box. Pilkie turned, "Come on little doggie; come on little doggie," and led the animal back to where he had found him".

Then peace came. Win Rolfe recorded how they heard at Sandling Place.

> "On a sunny day in May 1945 we all crowded in and around the messenger lobby, listening to an old wireless set as the voice of Winston Churchill proclaimed the end of the war in Europe"

The European war might have ended, but farming and food production were as vital as ever. German prisoners of war arrived to help on various Sandling farms. Bob Beeby told of those he had on Boarley Farm, coming in lorries all the way from a camp at Tonbridge. He got on well with them, they could be trusted and were very hard workers. At least one local lady also got on very well indeed with a certain handsome and fair-haired German.

Down by The Malta Jim Rogers had two p.o.w's who came at weekends to help him, and they would be rewarded with a nice dinner. One named Josef kept in touch, sending

The wages staff of Chatham Dockyard evacuated to Sandling Place.

letters and parcels from Germany. At Cossington Alan Veitch remembers Henry who was very nice and also kept in touch, but another had been in the Hitler Youth and was not so nice. George Brundle told Robin Walton that he had eight or nine p.o.w's and that they had an armed guard with them. Back at Boarley Fred Excell was very keen and learnt a few words of German.

And then there were the Italian p.o.w's, described by Bob as lazy, crawling into corn stooks at harvest time for a siesta. He called them "smoothies" and noted a mutual hatred between them and the Germans. Bob got the Italians organised to set up a new hop garden near Tyland Lane, which must have been an interesting contrast to their vineyards back home. They were an interesting diversion for Tyland Lane people, and John Bradford remembers them making slippers to sell, whilst Jack Rumble tells of them giving sweets to the local boys.

At the outbreak of war pupils and masters from Alleyns School at Dulwich were evacuated to the area, lodging with local families, including some at Sandling. Romance blossomed with local maidens, and as with the German p.o.w's wedding bells rang in a few cases. But the war years were deadly serious times. After Detling airfield had been bombed, a local man who had seen the destruction was so sure that an invasion was imminent that he gave his wife a pistol with instructions that if the Germans came "shoot the kids, and then yourself".

Was this tree planted to celebrate an earlier victory? And if so where? *(Gordon Fullagar)*

The White Horse Stone circa 1900.

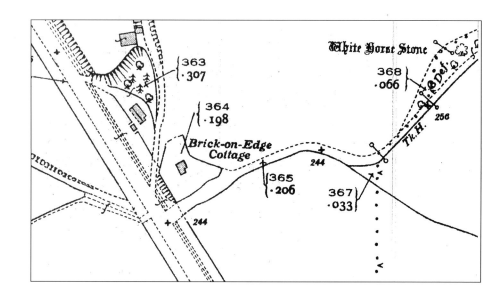

CHAPTER 24

Final Thoughts

Here is the opportunity to stretch the boundaries of Sandling just a little. On the northern edge, beside Pilgrims Way and close to where the High Speed Railway disappears underground, stands the ancient White Horse Stone, associated with legends of the Battle of Aylesford. Not far away and close to the garage at the foot of Bluebell Hill is the old Brick-on-Edge Cottage. It is said that either for the owner to save money, or for the builder to save effort, the bricks were laid on their edges so as to go further. Another theory is that a Brick Tax had been introduced, levied on the number of bricks used in a building. That also encouraged the use of a larger size of brick, and laying them on their edges was known as rat bonding. Brick-on-Edge Cottage is now much altered, and possibly only one old wall is now visible.

Pat Sandford's memories as a young lad have been related in several chapters. His family began running their lime business from Bluebell Hill in the 1860s, and what is now the Kits Coty Restaurant used to be their home. The lime kilns were in sight of Sandling and would be going day and night, with men alternating on twelve hour shifts. The flames rose high in the air.

Lime kilns at Bluebell Hill.

Going west along Forstal Road towards Aylesford you were still in the old Boxley parish, as witness a parish magazine of 1915 praising the Poole family who were living at 40 Forstal Cottages and having six men serving in the armed forces.

On the western edge of Cobtree Country Park and marked by a deep depression is the old worked-out claypit used for many years for brick making. This was originally by Aylesford Pottery and Brick Works, and their bricks stamped AP might still be found in local houses. A footpath passes close by the old claypit and at one point descends very steeply. This is where in Victorian times the miners would have made their way to work wearing clogs. The Pottery Arms pub close by Forstal Cottages was where the miners would go for refreshment, and Bob Corner remembers that the landlord Archie Beddowes used to spread sand on the floor as protection from the sticky clay which was brought in. Long after the mining had finished Archie through force of habit would still be spreading sand around, using a broom.

The bricks were taken on a tramway across Forstal Road and down to wharves on the Medway, from there to be transported by barge. In an article, Malcolm Shelmerdine wrote that both Garrard's little train at the zoo and its track were ex-quarry, and it would be no surprise if the local brickworks had been their origin.

Another simple rail track once ran from a large sandpit on the western side of Sandling Farm and down to another wharf. A footpath crossed the line and was carried over it by a simple footbridge supported by two brick piers. Large parts of these piers are

These barges are moored at Aylesford, but typify similar scenes at Cobtree Wharf.   (*Jim Sephton*)

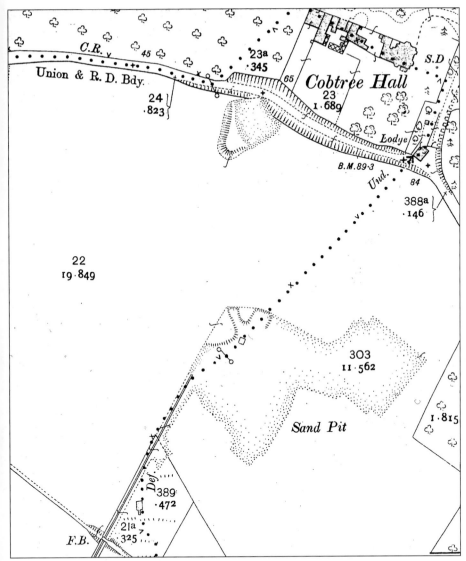

A 1908 map showing the tramway leading from the sandpit, then under the footbridge (FB) and on its way to the river.

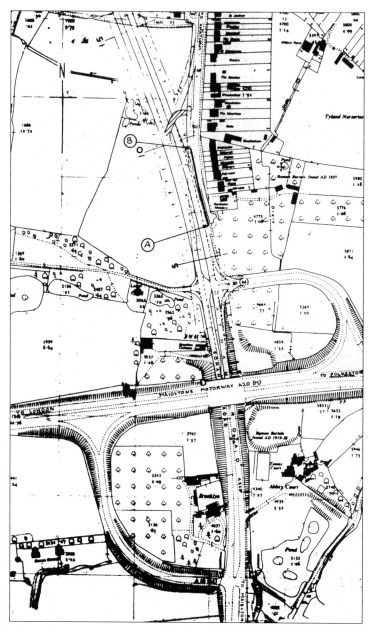

A 1969 plan showing how major roadworks transformed this part of Sandling.

still standing. They take some finding, being hidden in woodland at the western extremity of the Museum's land near the motorway. Working the sandpit seems to have finished by the 1920s, but the terrain was ideal for Garrard's show business contacts to come and film desert scenes, with his own camels very conveniently close at hand. The sandpit then became home for a building used by a horse-slaughterer Mr Dean until the late 1920s. This part of Sandling Farm was known for years afterwards by Bill Corner as "Deanys".

We have mentioned how roadworks have had a huge impact on Sandling life. Les and Linda Ellis move into Chatham Road on 1st October 1971 which was the very day that the new carriageway was opened and their stretch of Chatham Road closed up. The wide verges along Chatham Road indicate that widening there was once envisaged. There was for a time a junction linking the old and new roads but there were so many accidents that it was abandoned.

Up from The Running Horse is the short stretch of Old Chatham Road, now with houses running up above where the smithy used to stand. At the top you are at the back of the old Mill House, and you can glimpse the stream waters before they pass under the new carriageways.

And then the High Speed Railway came, causing environmental outage and personal distress in equal measure. Prominent amongst the many protesters was Rev. Joe Caley who travelled up to London to harangue Government officials.

The choice of schools for Sandling children was not always straight forward. Boxley School in the village had been opened in 1846, and for many years taught children from ages five to fourteen. Aylesford School may have been an option for some, but others would have walked to Boxley.

By the early 1900s Eastborough School in Union Street Maidstone was open, and that became the destination for older children. St. Paul's Infants School was an option for younger ones.

Northborough School in Peel Street opened in 1935 for Juniors and became an obvious destination for Ringlestone children and those close to the Chatham Road. Margaret McCarthy has reason to remember her time there, with Jack Rumble in the desk behind dipping her pigtails in his inkwell.

Eileen Hook understands that into the 1940s it depended upon which side of Deadman's Shaw in Tyland Lane you lived as to whether you went to Boxley School or elsewhere. Boxley School closed in 1945. In time Sandling School was opened, though ironically it was nearer Penenden Heath than Sandling's heartland.

Purpose-built rabbit warrens were introduced by the Normans as sources of meat and fur, and it is quite likely that the Abbey monks set up some in the area now known as Boarley Warren. It is no surprise that warrens produced rabbits surplus to requirements, and these surpluses could be sold as a commercial enterprise. In time beef and lamb became more widely available and warrens fell into disuse. But nature saw to it that there were still rabbits aplenty for those keen to catch them.

And so what changes Sandling has seen. Up until the First War any changes had been

2012 – Looking south with the sliproad from Tyland Barn bottom left.

An aeriel view of the rail route. Boxley tunnel in the foreground; Boarley Farm top right; Boxley Abbey near the bend of the motorway.

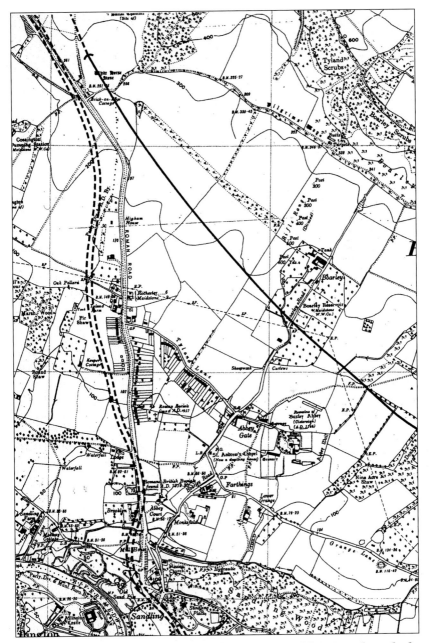

This 1947 map has been superimposed by Charles Luckhurst to show the later lines of the dual carriageway and the railway.

gradual. The 1920s and 1930s saw house building spread. The Second War interrupted things, but thereafter tractors and machinery came to replace horses and farm workers. Motor cars became invasive and much road-building arrived to accommodate them. Hop gardens and orchards disappeared. Families like the Mercers, Lushingtons, Ponders and Tyrwhitt-Drakes melted away, and military activity and museums replaced them. Hopefully this book may help to preserve memories of how things used to be.

The following people are amongst those who have contributed their memories, some sadly no longer with us.

Hilda Adams
John Allison
Tony Bathurst
Bob Beeby
Haydn Beeby
John Best-Shaw
Hermione Best-Shaw
James Best-Shaw
John Bradford
Walter Bishop
Margaret Caley
Roy & Eileen Carey
Mary Collins
Sylvia Coomber
Bob & June Corner
Rosemary Curtiss-Fuller
Don & Margaret Dracup
Edward Eckley
Les & Linda Ellis
Ian & Sue Flockhart
Jeff Friend
Gordon Fullagar
Amos Golding
Morwenna Hale
Mary Harvey
Vickie Harris
Eileen Hook
Chris & Susan Hunt
Danny Jarmann
Bernard Kirby
Betty Kirby
Peter Kirby
Liz Lampard
Jeremy Lawson
Bob Luckhurst

John Luckhurst
Charles Luckhurst
Ken Marshall
Nick McCabe
Pat McCabe
Margaret McCarthy
Molly Mitchell
Alan Moultrie
Elsie Muffett
Stuart & Dorothy Murray
Ann Nissen
Chris Norris
Brian & Babs Osborne
Elsie Parrett
David Rawlins
Raymond Relf
Dinah Reid
Andrew Rillie
Mick Rogers
Win Rolfe
Jack Rumble
Pat Sandford
Stanley Shrubsole
Brenda Steadman
Brian Tillman
Tommy Thompson
Jim Trousdell
Colin Vaughan
Alan Veitch
Olive Viggers
Maureen Waller
Robin Walton
Tony Webb
Richard Weller
Anna Wood